Teach Yourself
VISUALLY™

Search Engine Optimization

Visual™

Rafiq Elmansy

WILEY

John Wiley & Sons, Inc.

Teach Yourself VISUALLY™ Search Engine Optimization

Published by
John Wiley & Sons, Inc.
10475 Crosspoint Boulevard
Indianapolis, IN 46256

www.wiley.com

Published simultaneously in Canada

Wiley publishes in a variety of print and electronic formats and by print-on-demand. Some material included with standard print versions of this book may not be included in e-books or in print-on-demand. If this book refers to media such as a CD or DVD that is not included in the version you purchased, you may download this material at http://booksupport.wiley.com. For more information about Wiley products, visit www.wiley.com.

Library of Congress Control Number: 2013933937

ISBN: 978-1-118-47066-4

Manufactured in the United States of America

10 9 8 7 6 5 4 3 2 1

Trademark Acknowledgments

Contact Us

For general information on our other products and services please contact our Customer Care Department within the U.S. at 877-762-2974, outside the U.S. at 317-572-3993 or fax 317-572-4002.

For technical support please visit www.wiley.com/techsupport.

WILEY Sales | Contact Wiley at (877) 762-2974 or fax (317) 572-4002.

Credits

Acquisitions Editor
Aaron Black

Project Editor
Jade L. Williams

Technical Editor
Karen Weinstein

Copy Editor
Lauren Kennedy

Editorial Director
Robyn Siesky

Business Manager
Amy Knies

Senior Marketing Manager
Sandy Smith

Vice President and Executive Group Publisher
Richard Swadley

Vice President and Executive Publisher
Barry Pruett

Project Coordinator
Sheree Montgomery

Graphics and Production Specialists
Ronda David-Burroughs
Jennifer Henry

Quality Control Technician
Jessica Kramer

Proofreading
BIM Indexing & Proofreading Services

Indexing
Potomac Indexing, LLC

About the Author

Rafiq Elmansy (www.rafiqelmansy.com) is a worldwide author, designer, blogger, and SEO consultant. He is the owner of Pixel Consultation (www.pixelconsultations.com) for creative design and web marketing solutions. Rafiq has more than 12 years of experience in search engine optimization for Google and web marketing through social media networks such as Facebook, Twitter, StumbleUpon, and others.

Rafiq Elmansy owns a number of successful blogs in the design and photography field, such as Graphic Mania design magazine (www.graphicmania.net) and Photopoly (www.photopoly.net). Most of these websites and blogs have high SERP in Google search. His books and articles cover many topics including design, web marketing, blogging, and online business. Many of his writings are translated to different languages such as Japanese, Chinese, and Arabic. Rafiq is also a lecturer and speaker at events and online sessions about the web and technology.

Author's Acknowledgments

I would like to dedicate this book to my wife and my two daughters who fill my life with happiness, hope, and love. In addition, I would like to dedicate this book to my parents who lived and died with hope that I would become a good and helpful person. I hope I have achieved their expectations through my writings.

First, I would like to thank my wife for standing beside me throughout my life and the writing of this book. As a life and business partner, she has helped and motivated me in my SEO and web marketing career.

This book would not have been possible without the help and support of my Wiley team. I would like to express my deepest gratitude to acquisitions editor Aaron Black for his help from the development of the book through the final delivery. I cannot say thank you enough for his support and guidance on this project, especially in understand the series design.

In addition, I would like to express my sincere gratitude to my friend and project editor Jade Williams. Throughout the writing of this book, Jade provided tremendous help and support on a daily basis, providing suggestions, ideas, and encouragement in developing and carrying out this project.

I would like to express my deep acknowledgment to Lauren Kennedy, the copy editor, and Karen Weinstein, the technical editor, who dedicated a lot of effort and time editing the manuscript into a visual learning tool. In addition, I would like to express a special thanks to Kathleen Jeffers for her support and help on the administrative side of the project.

In summary, this book would have not come to life without the great support and help of my wonderful Wiley team to whom I owe the success of this project.

How to Use This Book

Who This Book Is For

This book is for the reader who has never used this particular technology or software application. It is also for readers who want to expand their knowledge.

The Conventions in This Book

❶ Steps

This book uses a step-by-step format to guide you easily through each task. **Numbered steps** are actions you must do; **bulleted steps** clarify a point, step, or optional feature; and **indented steps** give you the result.

❷ Notes

Notes give additional information — special conditions that may occur during an operation, a situation that you want to avoid, or a cross-reference to a related area of the book.

❸ Icons and Buttons

Icons and buttons show you exactly what you need to click to perform a step.

❹ Tips

Tips offer additional information, including warnings and shortcuts.

❺ Bold

Bold type shows command names or options that you must click or text or numbers you must type.

❻ Italics

Italic type introduces and defines a new term.

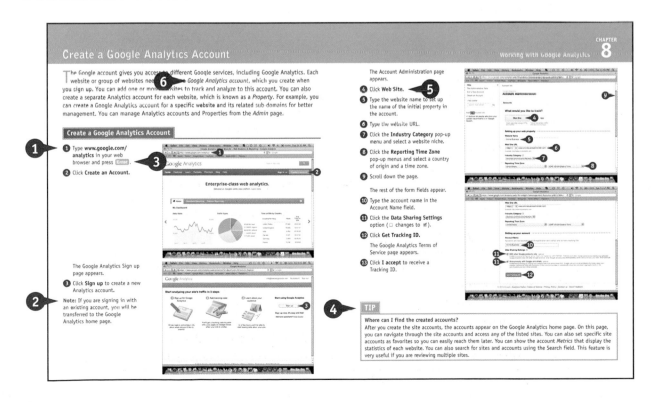

Table of Contents

Chapter 3 — Building an SEO Friendly Website

Chapter 4 — Mastering Keywords

Table of Contents

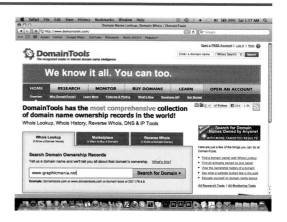

Chapter 7 Working with Content

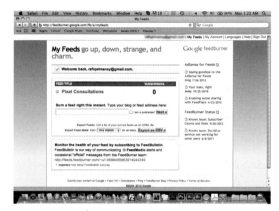

Chapter 8 Working with Google Analytics

Table of Contents

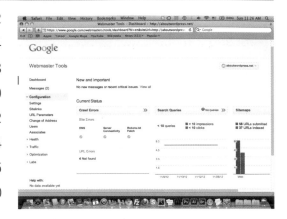

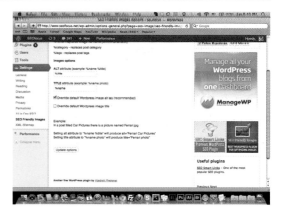

Table of Contents

CHAPTER 1

Understanding the SEO Process

When you have a website or a blog, most of your visitors find you using a search engine. The search engine user types his keywords or questions and the search engine displays the results from the indexed web pages that are relevant to the user search. Optimizing your website for search engines can help bring more traffic to your website and help it achieve better rankings in different search engines.

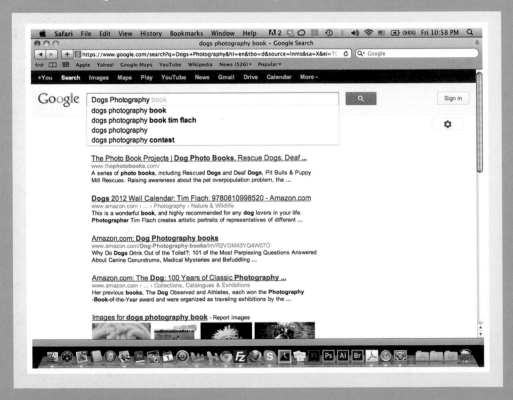

Introducing Search Engine Optimization

*S*earch Engine Optimization (SEO) refers to methods and techniques that you can apply to a website to increase its traffic, rank, and visibility in a search engine's results page. When you optimize your website, it has a greater chance of appearing in the search engine top results, which subsequently increases the traffic to your website. The optimization process includes many techniques and methods that are applied to the website itself or other sites that are related to the website content. Understanding the SEO process requires learning about how the search process works, the search page layout, and the different search engines that you target in the process.

Discover What SEO Is

Search Engine Optimization, SEO, is a process that you apply to a website to increase its rank and traffic from *organic search engine* searches. The process targets the free search, where users use any of the existing search engines, such as Google, Yahoo, and Bing, to search for a product, service, or information. It is different from a paid search, where the *webmaster* pays to appear at the top of the search pages, as discussed in Chapter 11.

Explore a Brief History of SEO

The process of optimizing web content first occurred in 1990, when search engines began indexing websites' content. It was much simpler than today, where website owners submit their sites to search engines. The search engines started and continue to use computer programs called *web spiders* or *crawlers* to crawl a website's pages and index them based on the site's niche and keywords. Early SEO was as simple as adding *meta* tags, which are HTML codes that include information about a website. Meta tags help search engines determine how the website content will be indexed using data such as the site's title, description, and keywords.

Look at the Google and SEO Relationship

With the launch of the Google search engine, the SEO process became more complex. It was developed to ensure better and more accurate indexing as well as identify the misuse of search engine optimization tactics such as keyword *stuffing*, which refers to including irrelative keywords in a web page to mislead the search engine crawlers. Then, Google started to refine the search technology by adding more factors for indexing and ranking websites. For example, *Off-page* optimization factors include external links to the website, and *On-page* optimization factors pertain to the website structure and content.

Apply SEO to a Website

The correct and standard use of search engine optimization techniques, which is known as *White Hat SEO*, helps put your site link at the top of the search engine results. Subsequently, this drives more traffic to your website and produces higher rankings. On the other hand, misusing search engine optimization techniques may negatively impact the site's indexing and ban it from appearing in the search engine results, which is known as *Black Hat SEO*.

YourSite.com: information you need
wwwyourslte.com › information › information you need

Compete Using SEO

With the ever increasing amount of content on the web, gaining visibility has become very competitive and it is harder to reach the top of the search engine pages and be easily identified by search engine users. Thus, this heavy competition makes optimizing your web content for the search engine a necessary process to ensure good indexing and a high ranking. SEO is an essential step after building a website, and as important as the website design and development.

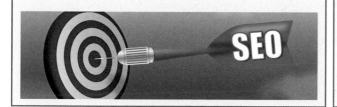

Explore SEO Resources

You can find many articles and resources on the web that cover the search engine optimization process. However, these articles alone will not give you a full understanding of the SEO process. While the articles provide tips and points of view, it is a good idea to use a structured guide such as this book along with hands-on practice and experience. This combination can help you gain a better understanding of the process and learn how to apply its different aspects to reach your search engine optimization goals.

Consider SEO Techniques

Search engine traffic is one of the greatest factors for success for your website, because you can turn this traffic into potential clients or website followers. The SEO process includes a number of techniques that you need to apply in parallel to move your website to the top of the search engine rankings and drive traffic to your website.

Search engine optimization techniques include different on-site and off-site strategies, which are known as On-page and Off-page optimization methods. Each type of method is very important and required to achieve successful SEO.

Apply On-page SEO

The On-page SEO techniques applied to the website itself make it search engine friendly. On-page simply refers to the optimization methods applied to the website or blog pages that will appear in the search engine results when the user types specific search terms. These methods are the first step in the optimization process when you are creating your website. Designing your website starts as early as when you are choosing your business or website name and identity. On-page SEO techniques include choosing a suitable domain name for the website, which is what users will type in their browsers to reach your website. It also includes creating the *meta tags* added to the HTML code that contain information about the website, such as its title, description, and related keywords, as well as optimizing the content heading, site content loading speed, keywords, site navigation, and site design structure. Although the On-page SEO techniques do not drive direct traffic to your website like the off-page SEO techniques, it makes the site content easier to reach by the search engine crawlers. It helps to categorize and index the site pages easier and faster than websites that do not apply these techniques.

Apply Off-page SEO

Unlike the On-page optimization techniques, the Off-page optimization techniques refer to the methods you apply outside the website to increase its rank, traffic, and visibility in the search engine. The methods are implemented and have either a direct or indirect impact on the website's traffic and its ranking in the search results. These methods may use third-party tools or websites such as directories and social networking websites to help build links to the website and improve traffic. The Off-page optimization includes link building, which refers to increasing the number of links that point to the website content. Off-page optimization also includes submitting your website to search engines and directories; and promoting it through press releases, articles, and more. You address Off-page methods after you apply On-page SEO and add content to your website. Both the On-page SEO techniques and the Off-page techniques are important to consider when you are optimizing your website. For example, you can use the website social network page on Facebook to drive traffic to a website, while at the same time, the website loads quickly, or the incoming user will leave the website without reading the content.

Discover Search Engine Optimization

The search engine optimization (SEO) process is an important part of your website business. Many website owners and webmasters wrongly believe that only the SEO process can do the magic and put their sites directly at the top of search results. However, the secret behind successful website SEO lies in your complete website management. Search engine optimization is much easier with high-quality websites than lower quality websites. Before I start talking about the SEO techniques, however, you should consider the following tips for getting better SEO results.

Target Your User, Not the Search Engine

When a visitor has a good experience on your website, he or she will return to the website because of its useful content. The number of returning visitors indicates the ratio of repeat visitors compared to new visitors.

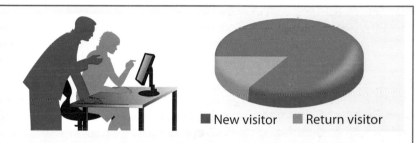

■ New visitor   ■ Return visitor

Even if you use good SEO, if the website content is poor, the results can be very disappointing; visitors who come to your website via search engines will not return again, which results in useless SEO efforts.

Assign Time Dedication

Optimizing your website is a long-term and ongoing process which takes a great deal of time and effort to see a significant impact on your website. Many website owners fail to achieve their SEO goals because they seek fast results. Planning for the SEO process

is covered in Chapter 13. However, before you start to learn about SEO techniques, remember that it takes time for search engines' crawlers to index your website content, which may take weeks.

Practice, Practice, Practice

The final tip to keep in mind when you are learning about SEO is that most of the methods covered in this book call for practice and analyzing the results. For example, some techniques are more suitable for specific website audiences than

others. So, you need to practice these SEO techniques, apply them to your website, analyze the results, and determine which ones help increase your website traffic and rank.

Understanding How People Use Search

Many users depend on search engines, especially Google, to find what they are looking for. When they do a specific search, they follow general steps beginning with the need to know information or about a service and ending with clicking the results. While having users complete the last step is the ultimate goal, it is important to understand how humans behave on the search page. This knowledge helps you figure out what users search for and how they search for it, and tailor your SEO process appropriately.

Search for Information

You can go to many places to search for information, such as search engines, the *Yellow Pages*, and newspapers. The statistics show that many people go to search engines to find information compared with other methods. This fact indicates the increasing

importance of targeting search engines and optimizing websites for it. Actually, many businesses have already started to focus on search engines to improve their websites' traffic and rank.

Using the Most Common Search Engines

Search engines use various methods and algorithms to index web content and display it in the search results page. This is one of the reasons users prefer a specific search engine. According to comScore, the market

share for search engines in 2011 places Google at the top of the search engines with more than 65% of the market share, and Yahoo is in second position with around 15%.

Begin Your Search

Users usually go through common steps while searching for information on the web. The SEO process starts when the user needs to search for specific information; for example, a user can be searching for local services or businesses. When you do a search

on a search engine, you usually provide a specific search query or a number of keywords, and the search engine provides results that you can choose from to obtain relative content.

Turn Your Need into a Search Query

When you do a search, you need to submit your request, or *search query*, as a word or group of keywords, known as *search strings*. The search engine uses these keywords to determine the results that best match your query and displays them in the search results page. In the SEO process, you focus on commonly used keywords when creating your On-page and Off-page optimization plan.

piano and violin • church works • oratorio and oper
divertimenti • ballets • concertos • pantomime
ind and vocal music • dain • serenades • chamber music
• keyboards • ensembles with voice and piano
ondo • allegro • horns • sin rings • Andanti

Mozart fragment recordings

Enter the Search Query into the Search Engine

The user types a request for information or a service as a search query, and then submits it to the search engine using the form that appears at the top of the search engine's web page. In this step, the user chooses between commonly used search engines. Most users use Google as their primary search engine because it loads easily, provides accurate results, and uses sophisticated methods to display the results that match the search query keywords.

London weather, October 2012

Search

View Search Results

The search results that appear on the search engine page are based on the keywords used in the search. These results depend on the crawlers that crawl the websites and index its keywords. The search results consist of two types, the *free search* results and the *paid search*, or *sponsored search*, results. Search engine page layout is covered later in this chapter in the section on understanding search page layouts.

London weather, October 2012 🔍

London Weather, October 2012 - forecast for the city
www.londonforecast
London Weather from 1909-2013...**Weather** for **October 2012**; 2013; 2014...average temperatures, record temperatures...See
Weather archives 1909-**2012**...October is wettest month...what to wear, public holidays, average temps

London in October - Weather 2012 - archived forecasts
www.londonweatherarchives
Weather Achives for **London** - 1887-2013...**2012** Jan, Feb, Mar, Apr...**October - Weather** archives 1887-**2012**...October events -
the month at a glance - **Weather** during historical events

Click a Specific Search Result

The user typically scans the search results that appear in the search engine page and reviews the titles and descriptions. If a result meets the user's needs and appears to be the best result, the user clicks it. Otherwise, the user reviews other results. The user can also use the search engine's advanced search options, such as filtering the results based on the date, the type of content, or specific search criteria.

Using Different Types of Searches

While there are different types of search engines, there are also different types of searches that users do when searching for information. The type of search a user does depends on the type of information he seeks from the search process and the query or the keywords he has submitted to the search engine. The three types are information queries, navigational queries, and transactional queries. Understanding the difference between them helps you determine the best combination of keywords to use to optimize your website content for your focused users and website visitors.

Using Informational Queries

The informational search query is used by users who seek specific information, such as the history of a specific country or scientific facts. An informational search usually returns a large number of results, especially when it is common information. In this case, it returns results from large information websites, such as Wikipedia, About.com, and Yahoo Answers. The results of this form of search can be links to websites, encyclopedias, forums, question and answers websites, discussion boards, or academic research PDFs.

London weather, October 2012 🔍

London Weather, October 2012 - forecast for the city
www.londonforecast
London Weather from 1909-2013...**Weather** for
October 2012; 2013; 2014...average temperatures,
record temperatures...See
Weather archives 1909-**2012**...**October** is wettest
month...what to wear, public holidays, average temps

London in October - Weather 2012 - archived forecasts
www.londonweatherarchives
Weather Achives for **London** - 1887-2013...**2012** Jan,
Feb, Mar, Apr...**October - Weather** archives
1887-**2012**...**October** events -
the month at a glance - **Weather** during historical events

Averages and Records - London Weather, October

Ads

Weather on call
www.weatheroncall
Get the latest **Weather,** road
conditions on your mobile...
London, Reading, Bath, Brighton

**London Weather - download
free app now**
www.weatherapps
Weather updates to your mobile
or computer...24 hour weather
forecasts...updated every 15
minutes. Get your free **London
Weather** app now

Using Navigational Queries

The navigational search query usually provides fewer, but more focused, results because the user does the search based on a company's name or a specific person's name. For example, the user can search a company name such as Samsung or Apple, or a historical figure such as George Washington. The results that appear for these types of queries usually show websites and profiles related to a company or person specifically or websites that have articles or news about them.

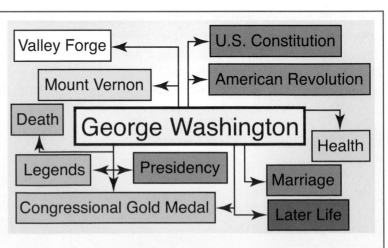

Using Transactional Queries

The transactional search query is an action-based search. When users do a search to buy a product, download a resource, or subscribe to a specific service, they are doing what is called a *transactional search*. Users who do this type of search are usually searching for products to buy, or services to use. For example, a user can search for website templates to buy or download. Or a user can search for travel or car rental services.

Search a Specific String

Many different types of users search for information on the Internet. The experienced user who has a full understanding of the search subject knows the best search term to use to find relative results. For example, the user may use a specific string query such as "How to create a High Dynamic Range image in Photoshop."

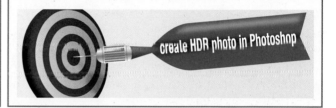

Search the Best Term

Sometimes the user knows what to search for, but cannot find the best term or the best keyword to use for obtaining optimal results from the search process. Therefore, the user navigates among the various results and tries to find the best link to click. For example, if the user is searching for information about High Dynamic Range (HDR) photography and does not know the best search query, the user can use the search term "How to create HDR photo effects."

Narrow Search Results

In this case, this user does not know what to search for or how to choose the search terms. So, the user simply types keywords to try to narrow the search results and gives clues about the information desired. For example, if the user does not know the best keyword to use when searching for HDR photos, the search term would be "How to create photos with color depth effect."

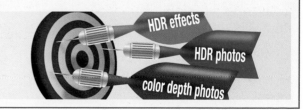

Understanding the Search Page Layout

Most of the search engines results pages have similar layouts on a desktop and laptop. At the top of the page is the query search box, where you submit or modify your search terms. At the bottom of the page is the *results information* that displays the number of results. In the center of the page, the *organic search* results display related content. In the upper-right of the page are the *paid search* results and advertisements. *Vertical search navigation* results focus on a specific topic, or filter results based on the search type. *Horizontal search navigation* filters search results based on criteria such as time.

Understanding the Search Page Layout

Use the Search Query Field

1. Type **http://www.google.com** in your web browser and press **Enter**.

2. Click in the search field.

3. Start typing a search term; for example, Adobe Photoshop.

The Google home page switches to the search results page.

4. Continue typing your search term.

5. Click **Google Search** (🔍).

Your search results appear on screen.

View Vertical Search Results

1 Type a search term in Google search; for example, Pablo Picasso.

2 Click **Google Search** (🔍).

The search results appear.

3 Click **Images** on the menu bar to display a related image search.

Images of your search appear on screen.

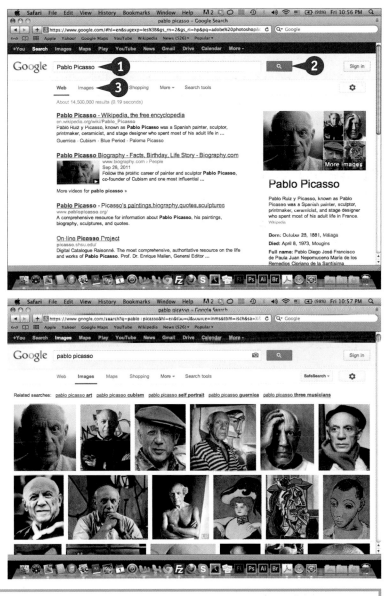

What are the different vertical search options?
The search for a specific type of media or information is an essential part of the search process. For example, you may need to search for only image results or video results. Thus, the search engine provides multiple vertical search options, such as image, video, maps, shopping, news, books, places, discussions, applications, and more.

Is the search layout different on mobile devices?
Yes, search page layout will appear different depending on the type of device the reader is using. If the reader is using a tablet or smartphone, the vertical search navigation will appear horizontally across the top of the screen in Google.

continued ▶

In addition to the vertical search, the search engine results page provides other tools and options you can use to narrow the results, such as the *horizontal search*. The horizontal search enables you to narrow your search results based on the properties of the search results. For example, you can filter your image search results based on publish date, size, and color. You can also filter video results based on duration, publish date, and quality. You can use these options to increase the quality of the results and reach better results by showing only the ones that meet with your search criteria.

Understanding the Search Page Layout (continued)

View Horizontal Search Results

1 Type a search term in Google search.

2 Click **Google Search** (🔍).

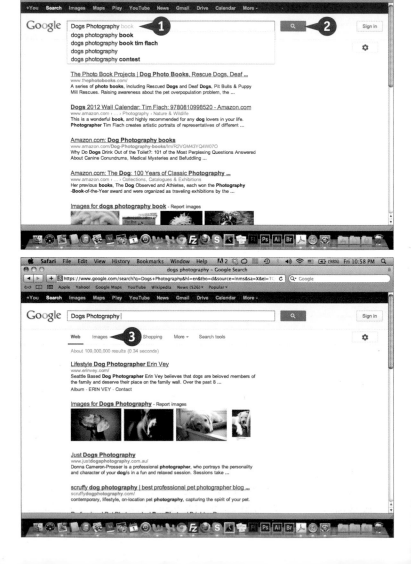

The search results appear.

3 Click **Images**.

The images search results appear.

4 Click **Search tools**.

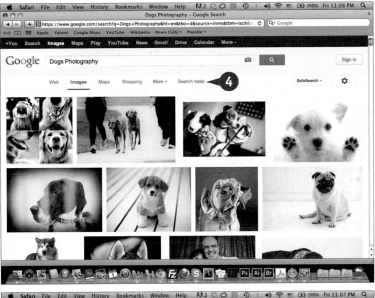

The search tools appear.

5 Click the **Any size** down arrow (˅).

Note: The Any size option does not appear on a smartphone device. You need to use desktop browser to see this command.

6 Click **Large**.

The image results with large sizes appear.

What are the related searches?

When you do not know the accurate search keywords, the search engine suggests more focused keywords, which are known as *related searches*. These keywords help you narrow the search results and allow you to reach results that better meet with your needs. The related searches depend on your search query keywords and common searches by other users.

Why should I use the horizontal search options?

The horizontal search allows you to filter results to display a specific image size or video length. For example, you may need to display videos that are short in length, or display only high-quality videos. When you optimize your media, you should consider how videos will display in your content in the search results.

Explore Different Search Engines

There are many search engines on the Internet, some of which share the same algorithm and techniques and others which have unique algorithms. In order to determine the search engines you need to target in your SEO plan, you have to understand how each search engine works and the potential traffic that you can receive from it. The major search engines include Google, Yahoo, and Bing. While Google is the most targeted engine in SEO, other search engines can provide traffic that can even affect your website Google rank in an indirect way.

Review the Google Search Engine

There is no doubt that Google (www.google.com) is the largest search engine, and its page rank algorithm formed the basic rules for early known search engine optimization. It was the first to rank indexed pages based on multiple factors and display these indexed pages based on their Google ranking. Google has an enormous number of servers located in countries worldwide, and having your website indexed by Google can help your website receive a lot of organic traffic. That said, many SEO techniques target putting websites at the top of Google rankings so they will appear at the top-most search position in the search results page, which is known as *Search Engine Results Page (SERP)*.

Review the Yahoo Search Engine

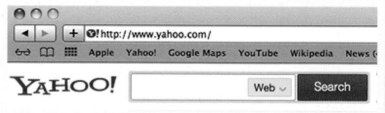

Yahoo (www.yahoo.com) has its own web crawler (Yahoo Slurp) and it uses different indexing capabilities to index your website. While Google focuses more on the concept of the search term and how users use different combinations of keywords, Yahoo focuses on the search keywords itself. Also, it places a lot of attention on the page title and Metadata. Understanding how the Yahoo search algorithm works will help you optimize your website or blog for Yahoo search. Also, Yahoo has its own paid directory, http://dir.yahoo.com/, where you can submit your website for indexing. Yahoo is now powered by Bing.

Review the Bing Search Engine

Bing (www.bing.com) is a popular Microsoft search engine. It is based on its predecessors, MSN and Live Search, which were old Microsoft search engines. The Bing algorithm places a greater focus on the web page title and description Metadata, similar to Yahoo. However, Bing has a better way to process queries and search terms than Yahoo. While major search engines take into account the authority of a link and the length of time a website has existed on the web, Bing is not restricted in this way. This is helpful to remember if you are building a new website, because Bing can index your website much more easily than Google, which puts the website domain name age as one of the important factors when indexing links and considering it trustworthy.

Review the AOL Search Engine

AOL (www.aol.com) is an old search engine. While AOL currently depends on Google to enhance the search results for those using AOL as their web searching tool, it depends on its own listing or external web links to display the search results. When you use AOL, you will notice that it provides both horizontal and vertical search as well as free search results and paid search results, which are promoted links that meet with your search criteria.

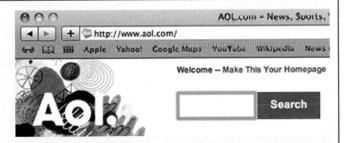

Review the Ask Search Engine

Ask (www.ask.com) is an old search engine with a different method of organizing a search. Ask groups the search results in a vertical search that can help the user narrow the search results. Ask is also a question and answer platform and allows users to ask questions and find answers from its own database. At this time, Ask is most focused on the Q&A search, which you will notice when you do a search on the Ask website. The results appear in the form of answers to your questions. While this may not affect your search engine optimization process, it can still drive traffic to your website if your content has been indexed by the Ask search engine.

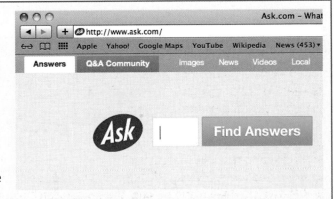

Set Up a Default Search Engine

Recent web browsers let you do web searches directly through their toolbars instead of visiting the search engine page first. This saves time and allows you to search the web using the browser search field in the toolbar or the website search field. Each web browser has a default search engine that opens and displays your search results. While most browsers use Google search, you can customize your web browser to do the search on other engines, such as Bing and Yahoo.

Set Up a Default Search Engine

① Click **Safari** ( ).

The Safari browser opens.

② Click **Start.**

③ Click **Preferences**.

The General Preferences dialog box appears.

4 Click the **Default search engine** pop-up menu and select Google.

5 Click **Close** (●).

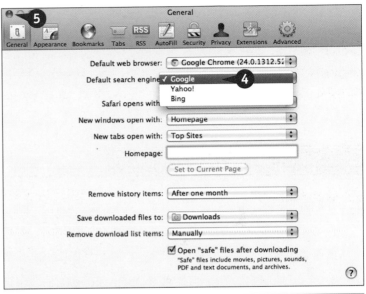

6 Type your search keywords in the search field.

7 Press Enter.

TIPS

Can I change the default search engine in other browsers?
Yes, you can change the default search engine in browsers such as Internet Explorer, Firefox, and Chrome. For example, you can go to the Chrome browser's Settings and select your preferred search engine from the Search section.

Can I make changes in Windows browsers?
Yes, the only difference is the location from which you choose your new search engine, depending on the version of Windows you are using. In Windows 8, you can change the search engine from the Manage add-ons screen.

CHAPTER 2

Preparing Your Website for SEO

Your website is the most important element in the search engine optimization (SEO) process. You can optimize a well-built website easily and it will get a high ranking by default. A poorly structured website may be impossible to optimize and your SEO efforts may not help it reach the top of the search engine results. Thus, it is important to prepare your website before applying any SEO steps.

Find a Website Niche

Before you start to build your website or choose the name, you have to determine your website niche or your business category. Finding the niche can help you to create a clear vision of the website's structure, content, and organization. Also, it will give you ideas about the type of visitors you will have and how to design the website and the content to meet their needs. Websites in some niches have to be built in a specific way, such as is the case for e-commerce and news websites.

Compare Focused and General Interest Websites

Typically, there are two types of websites: those that are focused and those that address a general interest. Focused websites center on specific topics, such as iPhone cases or design jobs. While these types of websites are easy to optimize for search engines because they focus on one topic, it is not always easy to achieve the required target, especially if the website is a niche website with few visitors. General interest websites, such as the buy-and-sell websites and news portals, include a variety of content from different sources, which makes it harder to optimize them. At the same time, they are not as risky as the focused websites because they include different content categories.

Focused VS **General**

Determine What Audiences Need

The audience or the website visitor is the most important factor that you have to consider when you design your website, build it, add the content, and optimize it for search engines. You have to understand the website visitors' needs and how they will interact with the website. This information can help you determine the best website structure and content to use.

Consider a Product Website Placement

E-commerce websites and websites selling specific products are focused sites that require a special consideration with optimization. You need to focus all your SEO tactics to help the website appear at the top of the search engine results when a user types a specific product name or related words in the search field.

Establish Your Website Content

Website content varies according to the purpose of the site and its business target. For example, content on e-commerce websites focuses on product information, reviews, and image previews for the product. Tutorial and training websites include articles, images, and video websites such as YouTube focus primarily on video content.

Generate Revenue

There are many ways to generate revenue from your website. One is to sell a product or service to website visitors, which is considered e-commerce. If your website gets a good number of visitors, you can also turn traffic into revenue by including advertisements with your content. Deciding how to get revenue from your website depends on multiple factors; for example, you need to consider how advertisements will impact visitors' satisfaction with your website.

Analyze Topics and Trends

To learn about different business niches and trends, you need to examine each niche with regard to people's interest. One useful tool for analyzing each niche is Google Trends. With this tool, you can type any keyword or topic that you would like to use on a website and find more information about global interest in the topic, the countries most interested in the topic, and the related keywords to this trend or topic. You can also narrow the results from the left menu and compare this keyword with other terms in the Search Term area.

Analyze Topics and Trends

1 Type **www.google.com/ trends** in your web browser.

2 Press **Enter**.

The Google Trends page appears.

Note: You need to sign in using your username and password, or create a new account if you do already have one.

3 Type **Online Business.**

4 Click **Explore.**

The keyword information appears.

5 Scroll to Regional interest.

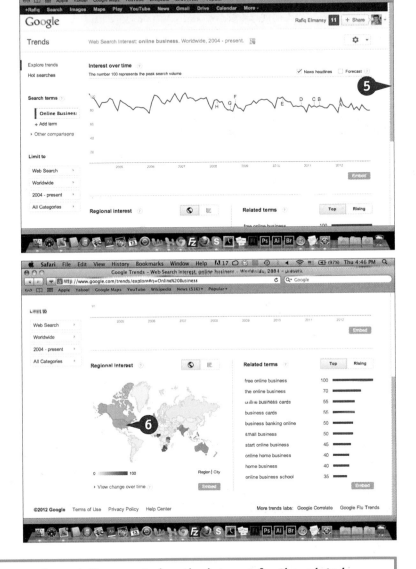

The map that shows the interest by region appears.

6 Click **United States** on the map.

The interest in the keyword United States appears.

How can I compare two or more search terms?
You can compare two or more search terms in the Search Terms section. Click **Add term.** Type the term you would like to compare and then press `Enter` to get a comparison between the terms on the map. You can use this option to compare two or more terms before choosing the term for your website.

How can I view the interest for the related terms?
You can view the related terms for your keyword at the bottom of the results page. When you click one of these related terms, you will be taken to a new results page, which shows global interest for the new term and different related terms.

Understanding Web Hosting

A web host is the online server or place where you upload your website files. The server is a computer with a special hardware configuration that enables it to save one or more website files. When a user types a website URL in the web browser, the server sends the website home page to the user. To understand how the website works, you need to learn basic hosting server terms and concepts, which you will use frequently when building your website and uploading it to the server.

Hosting Server Types

You can use several different types of hosting servers to host your website on the Internet. With *Shared Web Hosting,* many websites are located in one server and each website has its own patron on the server. This service is cheap and suitable for new websites that do not have many visitors. Once your website has a greater number of visitors, you can transfer your website files to a more professional server. A *Dedicated Server* is dedicated totally to one website, and the website owner should have strong networking skills to manage it. While it is expensive, it can handle large amounts of traffic and large numbers of files. A *Virtual Private Server (VPS)* is divided into small parts, which are known as *nodes*. VPS provides flexibility because you can increase the nodes when the website traffic increases.

Server Configuration

Storage, bandwith, and RAM are terms you should be familiar with when you search for servers or review different services. *Storage* refers to the storage capability of the website. You have to make sure that the hosting company will give you enough storage space to store your website files. An increase in storage size may lead to greater server costs. *Bandwidth* refers to the amount of traffic a server can receive. A larger bandwidth means that the server can receive more traffic. You need to make sure that the server provides enough bandwidth to be able to receive a lot of traffic, or provides a good upgrade plan to avoid any bandwidth-related problems in the future. *RAM* is the server's random access memory. It is used to handle different website files, such as JavaScript files and Personal Hypertext Preprocessor (PHP) programming language files that are used in creating dynamic websites.

Server Speed

The website speed refers to the server's ability to respond to visitors' requests by clicking links or loading pages. When visitors come to your website and find it loads slowly, they may leave and never visit again, unlike the fast websites. The server loading speed affects the visitors as well as the search engines that crawl your website to index its content. The search crawlers index the website content in a short period of time that can reach seconds. If your server is responding slowly to the search engine crawlers requests, the crawlers will leave the website without crawling all the pages. You can learn more about the server speed by reading customer reviews and feedback.

Server Security

Many new website owners do not give much focus to the website security issue, which can put them at risk of website hacking and *malware* scripts, which can infect your website and redirect traffic to other suspicious sites. The first important step in securing your website is to choose a secured server. While it is important to secure your website through using strong passwords, you need to make sure that the server is secure enough to prevent attacks on your website by applying methods such as a *firewall* that prevent malware attacks from reaching your website. You can learn more about the server security by reading customer reviews.

Managing Servers

To help you control your website server, the hosting server gives you a control panel, where you can create e-mails, and a database, which saves website information and content. You can also control different FTP accounts. One of the commonly used control panels is the *cPanel*, which is a web hosting control panel with a graphical interface and tools to make web server management easier. *Plesk* is another web hosting control panel that allows administrators to set up new websites, mail accounts, and more. In addition to the control panel, each server will have an *operating system*, which is the core system that runs the server. Most servers are either *Linux* based or *Windows* based. Some server packages allow you to add more than one website account on the same server, which is known as the *reseller package*.

File Transfer Protocol

File Transfer Protocol (FTP) is the technology you will need to upload the files to the server and access the server folders and files. You can use different programs to use this service, such as FireFTP and FileZilla. To access the server FTP, you should have an FTP URL, which will direct you to the FTP folder on the server, and the FTP username and password. You can create an FTP account from the server control panel or ask customer support to create one for your site. Usually, the FTP allows you to access a specific directory or the main folder of the server, which includes the website files, also known as the *root folder*. There are many names for the root folder, such as `public_html` and `home`. The root name can change depending on the type of server control panel.

Website Related Terms

Before you start using the hosting server, you want to get familiar with some important terms. *IP Address (Internet Protocol Address)* is a unique number that is used to identify devices and websites that connect to the Internet. It consists of four sets of numbers, separated with dots and ranging from 0 to 255. Its format looks like 90.120.100.50. *URL (Uniform Resource Locator)* is a web address that you type in the web browser to reach a website. It is usually mapped to the website IP. *Name servers* are server-side URLs added to the domain registrar that provide the URL to connect the website with the server. *Sub-domain* refers to the sub-sites of the main website. For example, the website can be http://www.website.com, and the sub-domain is http://sub.website.com.

Choose a Web Host

One of the most important steps before you start building your website is choosing a trusted hosting service company. You can find many hosting companies on the Internet. Take time to learn about each company and read the reviews on the companies. The hosting company should provide uptime for the website at all times, which is known as 99% uptime. You do not want your website to go down when users try to visit it. You also need to make sure that the server company provides reliable customer support. A good resource to learn about different hosting companies is at www.findmyhosting1.com.

Choose a Web Host

1 Type **www.findmyhosting1. com** in your web browser.

2 Press **Enter**.

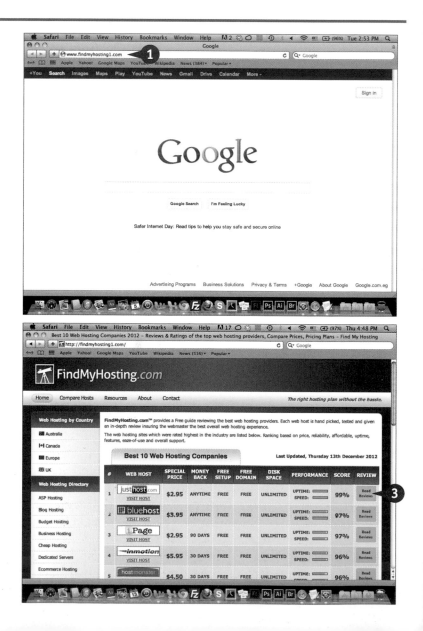

The home page appears with an updated list of the top 10 best web-hosting companies.

3 Click **Read Reviews.**

The hosting company reviews appear.

4 Scroll down to User Reviews.

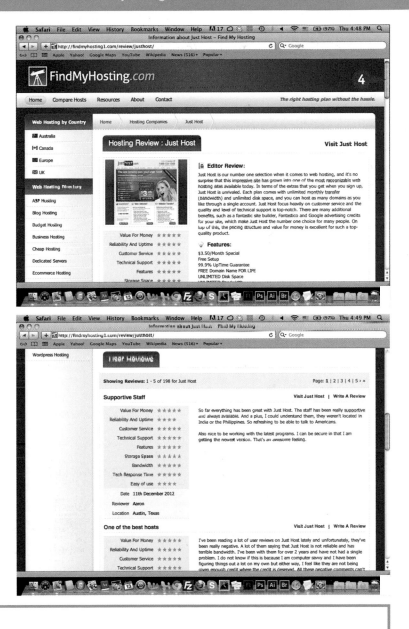

The user review appears.

TIP

What are the free hosting services?

Some companies provide free hosting services that allow you to create your website. Many of these companies provide services you can use to create blogs or websites that you can update frequently and use to create archived content. While these hosting services are limited in resources and configuration options, they are useful for beginner website owners who would like to use them as a tool to learn how website building works. Some examples for these free hosting websites are www.wordpress.com, www.blogger.com, http://www.squidoo.com, and https://www.tumblr.com. Free hosting services are not recommended for SEO, because you need to have your own website hosting server and URL as an initial step.

Choose the Website Domain

The domain name is the URL that people use to access your website. It is also the first thing that the search engines check when accessing your website. Choosing the domain name is a very critical task because it is not changeable. So, you have to choose an effective name that reflects the website content. Also, it should be easy to remember and include the important keywords in the website for better SEO results. There are many domain registrars that you can use when you are searching for domains and then buying them, such as GoDaddy and Network Solutions.

Choose the Website Domain

1. Type **www.godaddy.com** in your web browser.

2. Press `Enter`.

The GoDaddy website appears.

3. Type a domain name, for example homemotherjobs.

4. Click the pop-up menu and click **.com.**

5. Click **Search.**

The domain availability page shows the domain is available.

6 Click **Add.**

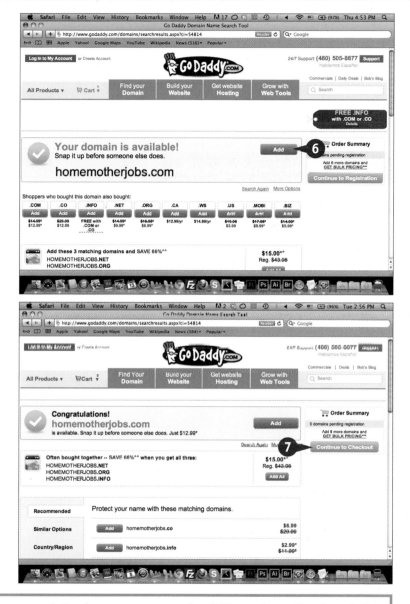

The domain is added to the shopping cart.

7 Click **Continue to Checkout.**

You can follow the next steps to complete registering the domain name.

TIPS

What is the Top Level Domain (TLD)?
The Top Level Domain (TLD) is the last part in the URL after the period, indicating the highest level in the hierarchical Domain Name Systems (DNS). Many TLDs have different types and uses. For example, .COM refers to commercial websites, .NET to networks, .ORG to organizations, and .TEL to communication.

For how many years should I purchase the domain?
Most new website owners buy a domain for one year and then renew it. While this is useful for beginners, the search engines give more credit to websites that are registered for three years or more. More years indicate the website owner has a strong desire to continue with the website and develop more content through the years.

Create a Privacy Policy Page

The privacy policy is a website page that includes information about website policies, how the website collects information, and how it deals with collected personal data, such as names and e-mails. Adding a privacy policy is an indicator that the website is professional and respects visitors' information. It is also very important in SEO, especially for Google indexing. You should have a privacy policy page to indicate that your website is reliable. While you can write your own privacy policy, there are websites that can help you write one, such as www.easyriver.com/myprivacy.htm.

Create a Privacy Policy Page

1 Type **www.easyriver.com/ myprivacy.htm** in your web browser.

2 Press **Enter**.

The Create your Privacy Policy page appears.

3 Type the website name.

4 Type the website e-mail address.

5 Click here to select the website's intended age range or select to exclude this clause.

6 Type your feedback about the privacy policy generator service.

7 Type your e-mail address.

8 Scroll down to the end of the page.

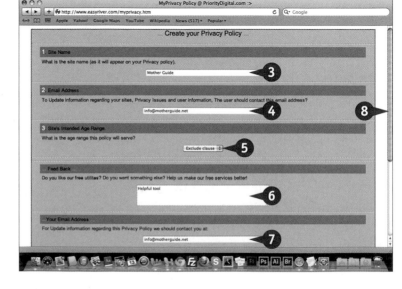

The end of the page appears.

9 Click **Create my Privacy Policy.**

The privacy policy text appears.

10 Copy the Privacy policy code to add in a HTML document to create the privacy policy page.

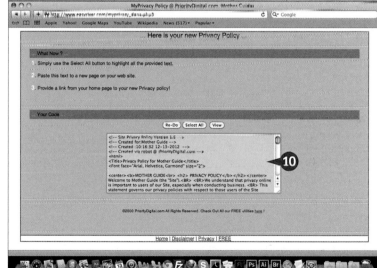

What should the privacy policy page include?
The privacy policy page should include information about your website, why it needs to collect information from the users, the type of information being collected, and the purpose. The privacy page should also include information about the security of the collected data and information sharing with third-party sites and site members.

Are there other free privacy policy generators?
Yes, there are many free generators that you can use to create your website privacy policy. For example, you can use www.freeprivacypolicy.com to create the privacy policy code and then copy and add it to your website HTML code. This service allows you to generate only one free privacy policy.

Create Website Forms

When you build your website, it is important to create a way for website visitors to interact with you and contact the website team for inquiries and issues related to the website. While this does not have direct impact on the SEO process, it can be helpful when your website reaches a good position on the search engine results page, and when others need to contact you for advertising opportunities and collaboration. You can have many embedded contact forms on the website, or use external contact forms that are provided for free, such as www.phpform.org, which lets you create different types of web forms.

Create Website Forms

1 Type **www.phpform.org** in your web browser.

2 Press **Enter**.

The form builder page appears.

3 Select a form color.

4 Click **Next.**

5 Click form objects to build the form.

6 Click **Untitled Form.**

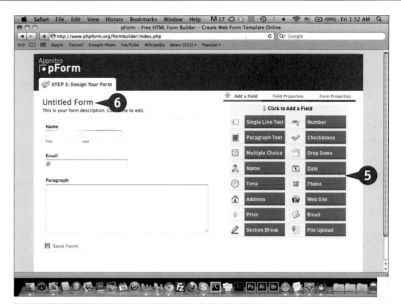

The form properties appear.

7 Type the form title.

8 Type a form description.

9 Click **Save Form.**

After saving the form, you can download and add it to your website HTML file.

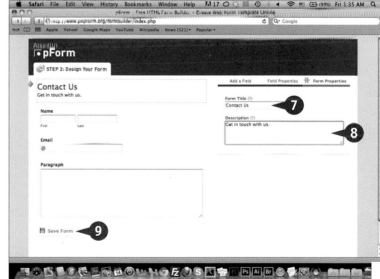

How can I embed the contact form in the web page?

To add the form inside your page and allow users to send messages directly through your website, you need to embed the form code in your website HTML code. You can learn about how to create a web form from this link www.w3schools.com/html/html_forms.asp.

Where can I find additional free places to create web forms?

You can find and create web forms at www.123contactform.com. You can also find free form builders that will help you to create different types of forms, such as the reports, contacts, and payments forms at www.emailmeform.com and www.myjotform.com.

Check Browser Compatibility

A fter you build your website, it is important to make sure it appears properly in different browsers so site visitors can see it and navigate through it without any errors or problems. In large companies, testing teams handle this. But individuals and developers can only test their websites through a couple of browsers on their personal computers. Therefore, it is important to test your website on different operating systems and browsers. http://browsershots.org is one of the websites that allows you to see how your website will look on a wide variety of browser versions and operating systems.

Check Browser Compatibility

1 Type **www.browsershots.org** in your web browser.

2 Press **Enter**.

The Browser Shots page appears.

3 Type your website URL.

4 Select the desired browser types and versions.

5 Click **Submit.**

The screenshot results appear.

6 Click a screenshot.

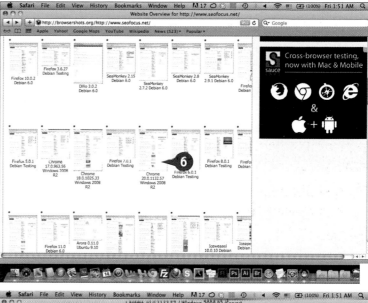

The screenshot is maximized.

How do I check the website compatibility on different browsers?
To perform a complete testing of your website, you have to check the website on different browsers and different versions for each browser. Also, you need to check the website on different operating systems and devices to ensure an optimal view and easy navigation of the content on different screen sizes.

What are the other browser check websites?
Cross Browser Testing is another browser checker service that you reach at www.crossbrowsertesting.com. Cross Browser Testing provides live testing for your website with support for creating multiple screenshots and using mobile testing to make sure that your website is working properly on mobile devices.

Check Your Website with Adobe BrowserLab

Adobe BrowserLab allows you to test websites on different browsers. You can access Adobe BrowserLab with your Adobe ID, or you can create one. In the Adobe BrowserLab, enter the URL that you would like to test in the left field and then set the number of screen views on the right. You can set a different browser for each part of the screen. Once you are done, you can click the Refresh button to display the website for each screen part. You can scroll and review the website page.

Check Your Website with Adobe BrowserLab

1 Type **browserlab.adobe.com** in your web browser.

2 Press **Enter**.

The Adobe BrowserLab page appears.

3 Click **Start using BrowserLab.**

The Adobe BrowserLab login page appears.

④ Type your username.

⑤ Type your password.

⑥ Click **Sign In**.

Note: You can create a new account if you do not have one.

The BrowserLab page appears.

⑦ Type the website URL that you would like to test.

⑧ Click the **Number of Screen Views** pop-up menu and select 2-Up View.

⑨ Click the **Browser** pop-up menu and select Internet Explorer 9.0 - Windows.

⑩ Click the other **Browser** pop-up menu and select Safari 5.1 - OS X.

⑪ Click **Refresh** (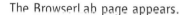).

The website displays for each screen in both the Explorer and Safari browsers.

TIP

What is different between Adobe BrowserLab and other checkers?

The Adobe BrowserLab is made to allow designers and developers to check the compatibility of their websites that depend on Adobe technologies, such as Adobe Dreamweaver and Adobe Muse. Adobe BrowserLab does not provide multiple screenshots for the different browsers to use to check websites; however, it allows you to move around the currently tested page, and click the page links. In addition to the current view, Adobe BrowserLab can divide the page into four labs.

Check Your Website with Screenfly

Website visitors can come from different devices, such as smartphones and tablets. Each device has a web browser that displays the website in a specific size. Obviously, it is important that your website displays correctly for different users; therefore, you need to test how your website looks on different devices and screen sizes. Screenfly from QuirkTools lets you do this. You simply type your website's URL in the test field and you can see what it looks like on different screen sizes. This way you can make sure that your website looks good on a variety of different devices.

Check Your Website with Screenfly

① Type **http://quirktools.com/ screenfly** in your web browser.

② Press **Enter**.

The Screenfly tool appears.

③ Type the website URL in the field.

④ Click **Go.**

The website preview appears.

5 Click **Tablet.**

The tablet browser sizes appear.

6 Click **Apple iPad 1&2.**

This displays a preview of the website in the selected size.

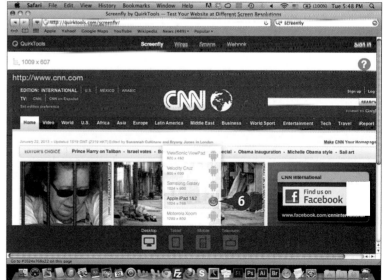

What test sizes are available in Screenfly?
Screenfly tests your website based on the current size of the web browser window. The browser size appears at the top left of the Screenfly interface. On the bottom of the page, you can change the view based on the device; options include Desktop, Tablets, Mobile, and Television.

Are there other tools for checking how a website appears in different browsers?
Yes, additional tools are available to test your website on different browsers. You can use the Resolution Test add-on with the Chrome browser available at https://chrome.google.com/webstore/detail/resolution-test-idhfcdbheobinplaamokffboac cidbal?hl=en.

CHAPTER 3

Building an SEO Friendly Website

The SEO process starts with building your website as it should be optimized, so the search spiders can crawl it and index its content once it is published on the Internet. The SEO preparation steps include creating the website structure, ensuring easy crawling, establishing the correct links hierarchy, and avoiding any errors that might prevent search engine indexing.

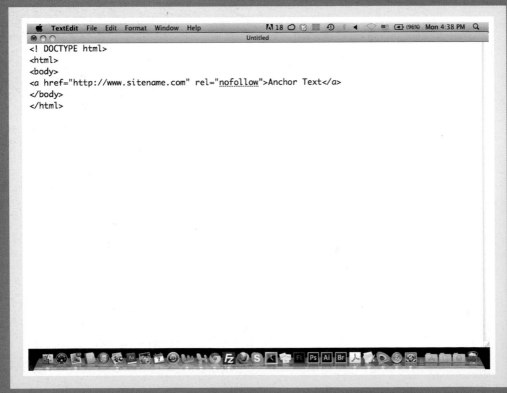

```html
<! DOCTYPE html>
<html>
<body>
<a href="http://www.sitename.com" rel="nofollow">Anchor Text</a>
</body>
</html>
```

Plan for an Optimized Website

You have to consider your SEO methods even before you start to build your website, because optimization affects every part of your website, including its design, development, functions, and structure. If you do not take the methods for optimizing website content and files, known as *On-page SEO*, into consideration early on, it may be difficult to optimize your website in the future because many of the On-page SEO relates to the website infrastructure itself.

User-Friendly Functions

It sounds strange to talk about usability as the term is more related to the design side of the site developing, but actually, it is very important because once visitors locate what they need on a website, they remain on the website for a longer time. If users are satisfied with the website, they will save it as a *Favorite* and return to it again. If they find your website hard to use and they cannot find information easily, you will never be able to keep them on the site, even if you use every possible SEO tactic.

URL Structure

When you build a website, you should name your HTML files so it is easy for the search engine to identify the keywords and the file categories. For example, if you have a page that talks about photography basic tips, you can name the HTML file basic-photography-tips. html, and visitors can reach it through www.sitename.com/basic-photography-tips.html. This can help search engines index the web page and display it for users when they type photography tips in the search field.

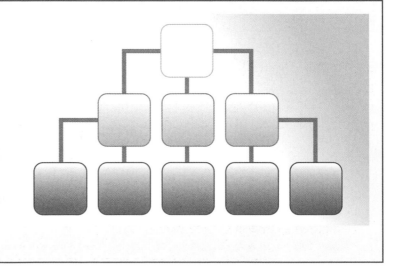

Website Design Structure

One of the important things to consider is the website design. The clean design with optimized images can load fast and search engines can crawl it faster than a website with large-sized images, which take a long time to load. Also, a flexible design that can be modified easily allows you to customize your website based on the SEO recommendations.

Website Navigation

Navigation is very important to search engines, and website pages should be linked to each other so users can easily reach any page on a website from the other pages on the site. A web page that does not allow you to navigate to other pages on the website is called a *dead link*, and dead links are a bad practice in the SEO industry. The best way to unify your website pages is to create a menu that is located on each web page that visitors can use to link to other pages within the website.

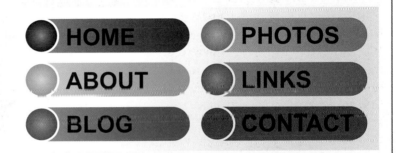

SEO Website Functions

When you build your website, you have to consider functions that help the SEO process. For example, you can add a section under each post or content area that tells users about related topics on the website. Then they can visit the content for the related topics and get more information. This can help increase your website page views and the time users spend on your website.

Lorem ipsum dolor sit amet, consectetur adipisicing elit, sed do eiusmod tempor incididunt ut labore et dolore magna aliqua. Ut enim ad minim veniam, quis nostrud exercitation ullamco laboris nisi ut aliquip ex ea commodo consequat. Duis aute irure dolor in reprehenderit in voluptate velit esse cillum dolore eu fugiat nulla pariatur. Excepteur sint occaecat cupidatat non proident, sunt in culpa qui officia deserunt mollit anim id est laborum.
Related topics - click here

Create a Website Sitemap

The sitemap is an XML-based file that indexes the website's links, images, and files. It should follow the same structure as the website. The sitemap file is usually named *Sitemap.xml*, *Sitemap.html*, or *Sitemap.php* and it is placed in the website server so the search engines can reach it directly by following the website link; for example, it can be www.*sitename.com*/sitemap.xml, where sitename.com can be your own website name. While you can create the sitemap manually, there are tools you can use to create a sitemap for your website without needing to learn how to write XML code, such as the free sitemap generator at www.xml-sitemaps.com.

Create a Website Sitemap

1 Type **www.xml-sitemaps.com** in your web browser and press **Enter**.

The XML Sitemaps website appears.

2 Scroll down to the form.

The XML sitemap form appears.

3 Type the website URL.

4 Click the **Change frequency** pop-up menu and select the website update frequency.

5 Click the **Last modification** date option (○ changes to ◉).

6 Click the **Priority** option to select how the XML sitemap calculates the URL's indexing (○ changes to ◉).

7 Click **Start.**

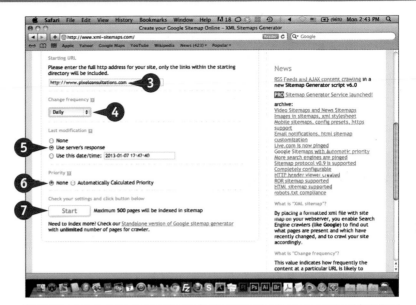

The website XML sitemap is created.

8 Click the link to download it.

After downloading, you can upload the sitemap to your website server root folder.

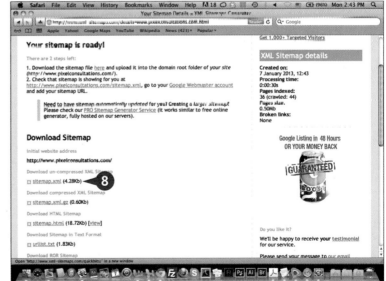

TIP

What are the different types of sitemaps?
There are different types of sitemaps that you can create and upload to the website server. Each of these XML sitemaps can contain specific types of links. The XML sitemap can include an image sitemap, which contains links for the images in the website and its information. Also, there are video sitemaps, news sitemaps, and mobile sitemaps. You can upload multiple XML sitemap files to the same website and submit these sitemaps to search engines to ping the search engines to crawl and index them. When you add new content to the website, you have to update the sitemap with the new added content.

Create a Robots.txt File

The *Robots.txt* file is a text document that informs the search engine spiders which parts of your website you would like to be crawled and which parts you do not want the search engines crawling. For example, if you have large source files, crawling them may overload the server and consume the search engine crawlers' time indexing website files. You can create the Robots.txt file using text editors, such as TextEdit for the Mac and Notepad for Windows.

Create a Robots.txt File

Create a File

1 Click the **Finder** icon (🖐️).

The Finder window opens.

2 Click **Applications.**

The installed applications appear.

3 Click **TextEdit.app.**

Note: For Windows users, you can click **Start**, click **All Programs**, click **Accessories**, and then click **Notepad.**

The text editor opens.

4 Type **User-Agent:*.**

5 Press Enter.

6 Type **Disallow: /video/.**

7 Press Enter.

8 Type **Disallow: /sources/ sources/.**

9 Press Enter.

10 Click **File.**

11 Click **Save.**

The Save As dialog box appears.

12 Navigate to the location where you want to save the file.

13 Type a name for your file in the Save As field, or in the File name field if you are using Microsoft Notepad.

14 Click **Save.**

The file saves.

TIPS

What does User-Agent reference?
The User-Agent describes which search engine should follow the rules after it. When you set it to *, this means it is applied to all the search engine robots.

What are the Allow and Disallow rules?
Allow and Disallow set the rules for the search engine spiders to crawl specific folders on the server or exclude others. Usually, you use Disallow to prevent the search engine spiders from crawling specific folders on the server; all other folders will be crawled by default.

continued ▶

Create a Robots.txt File (continued)

After you create the Robots.txt file, you need to upload the file to the server. Usually, the Robots file is uploaded to the main folder on the server using a technology called *File Transfer Protocol (FTP)*. FTP applications upload files to the website server using the username and password the server administrator or hosting company provides. There are many FTP clients such as FireFTP and FileZilla along with the FTP URL.

Create a Robots.txt File (continued)

Upload the File to a Server

15 Click the **FileZilla** icon ().

Note: If you do not have FileZilla on your computer, you can download or install it from http://filezilla-project.org.

The FileZilla client appears.

16 Click the **Site Manager** icon (📋).

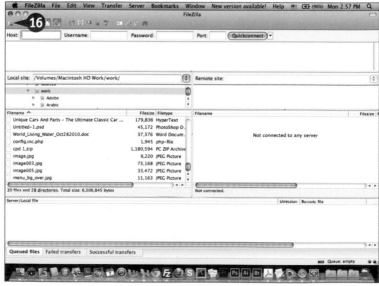

The Site Manager appears.

Ⓐ If your new site form is unavailable, you can click **New Site** to display it.

⑰ Type the FTP URL in the Host field.

⑱ Click the **Logon Type** pop-up menu and select Normal.

⑲ Type a username.

⑳ Type a password.

㉑ Click **Connect.**

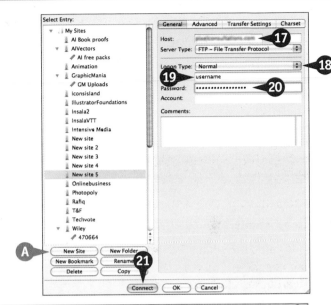

The FTP folder on the server appears.

㉒ Click and drag the robots.txt file to the FTP side to upload it.

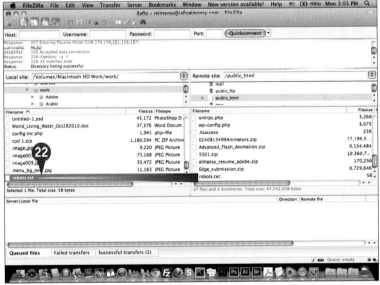

Using the Nofollow Attribute

The Nofollow attribute is an HTML snippet that is added to the hyperlink code that creates links in websites. The Nofollow attribute plays an important rule in SEO, especially in building links that impact the website rank. Usually, the links to external websites can reduce the rank of the website. Therefore, you use the attribute `rel="nofollow"` in your HTML code to tell the search engine not to follow this link and discard it when evaluating the website. You can type this code in any text editor, such as TextEdit or Notepad, and save it as an HTML file.

Using the Nofollow Attribute

① In your TextEdit file, type **<a href="www.sitename.com" rel="nofollow">Anchor Text</a>** on the line following the `<body>` tags.

Note: For Windows users, you can write the code in Notepad.

② Click **File.**

③ Click **Save.**

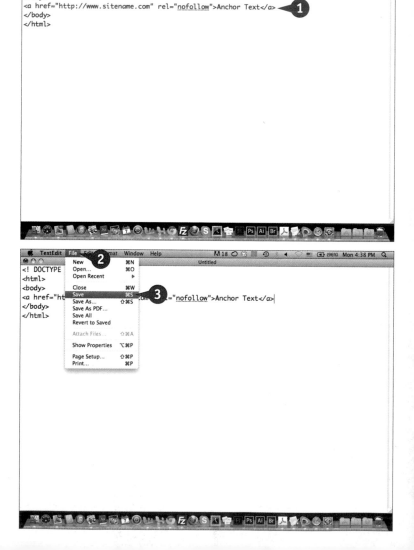

The Save As dialog box appears.

④ Navigate to the location where you want to save the file.

⑤ Type the name of the file in the Save As field, or in the File name field if you are using Microsoft Notepad.

⑥ Click **Save.**

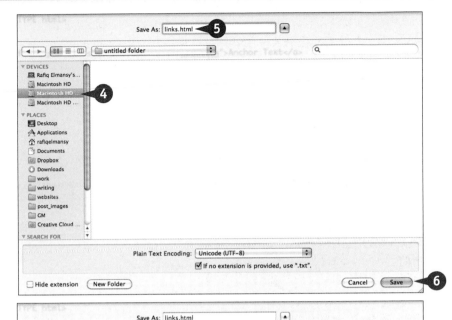

An alert message appears.

⑦ Click **Use .html.**

The file is saved as an HTML file. You can view the file using your web browser.

TIPS

Does the Nofollow attribute violate Google rules?
There are rumors that Google does not allow the Nofollow attribute because it prevents passing the website rank from one site to another. This is wrong. Google introduced the Nofollow attribute in 2005. Then the Yahoo and Bing search engines started to use it in their algorithms.

How do I use the Nofollow attribute in SEO?
In many cases, you will want to add external links to your website as part of the information you provide to visitors. While this data is helpful, the reader does not care about the search engine crawler and how it follows the links. So, you can use the Nofollow attribute with these links to avoid a drop in your website rank.

Build an .htaccess File

The .htaccess file is uploaded to the website server to help you control the web server's behavior. It can help protect your website from specific issues, such as accessing secured directories on the server and banning unwanted visitors from specific sources. You can upload the .htaccess file to the website's main folder on the server or any other folder that you would like to apply .htaccess rules to. While the file has a strange extension name, .htaccess, you can create it by using any text-editing application.

Build an htaccess File

1 In your TextEdit or Notepad editor, type **RewriteEngine On** to enable rewrite of the search engine rules.

2 Press Enter.

3 Type **RewriteCond %{HTTP_ USER_AGENT} ^WGET [OR]** to prevent retrieving information from your server.

4 Press Enter.

5 Type **RewriteRule ^.* - [F,L]** to rewrite the access rules.

The basic htaccess file is created.

6 Click **File.**

7 Click **Save.**

The Save As dialog box appears.

8 Navigate to the location where you want to save the file.

9 Type **.htaccess** in the Save As field, or in the File name field if you are using Microsoft Notepad.

10 Click **Save.**

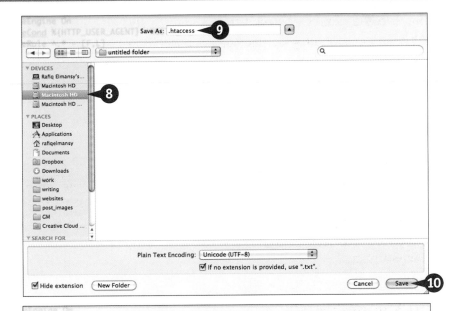

An alert message appears.

11 Click **Use ".".**

After you save the file, you can upload the .htaccess to your server root.

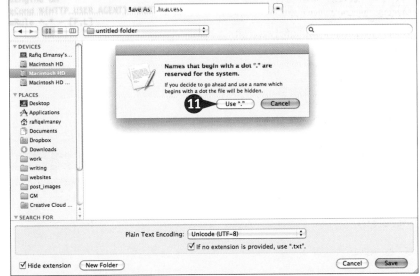

TIP

Is there a tool to help me to create the .htaccess file?
Yes, if you find writing the .htaccess complex, you can use tools to help you build the .htaccess file at www.htaccesstools.com. The www.htaccesseditor.com/en.shtml site enables you to choose from different rules. The http://www.yellowpipe.com/yis/tools/htaccess_generator/index.php site enables you to create .htaccess and .htpasswd that are used to protect special directories on your server.

Protect Website Images with .htaccess

You can use the .htaccess file to prevent others from linking to your website's images. To do this, you add code to the .htaccess file, which allows images to link only from your own website. This code is `RewriteCond %{HTTP_REFERER}!^http(s)?://(www\.)?yourwebsite.com [NC]`, which allows only your website to link to the images with specific formats. These format are defined in the next code line: `RewriteRule \.(jpg|jpeg|png|gif|flv|swf)$ - [NC,F,L]`.

Protect Website Images with .htaccess

1 In the .htaccess file, press `Enter` after the `RewriteEngine On` line.

2 Type **RewriteCond %{HTTP_REFERER}!^http(s)?://(www\.)?yourwebsite.com [NC]**, replacing *yourwebsite.com* with your website name.

3 Press `Enter`.

4 Type **RewriteRule \.(jpg|jpeg|png|gif|flv|swf)$ - [NC,F,L]**.

The new rules are added.

5 Click **File.**

6 Click **Save.**

The Save As dialog box appears.

7 Navigate to the location where you want to save the file.

8 Type **.htaccess** in the Save As field, or in the File name field if you are using Microsoft Notepad.

9 Click **Save.**

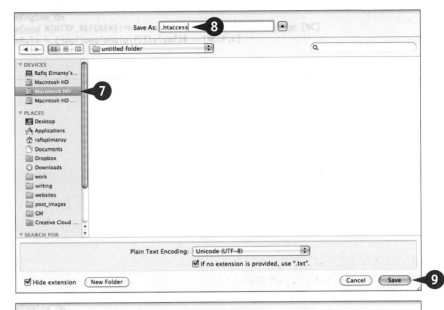

An alert message appears.

10 Click **Use ".".**

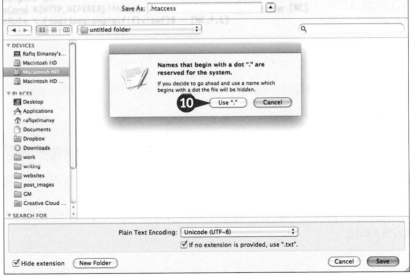

TIPS

What is image hotlinking?

An *image hotlink* refer to sites that link to images on your website without uploading the images directly on their servers. This can consume bandwidth and cause server load. The .htaccess protection code can help you avoid this problem.

How do I prevent unwanted traffic?

You can use the www.htaccesstool.com website to generate an .htaccess code that allows you to block incoming traffic from certain IP addresses. Monitor your website statistics to make sure that you do not have excessive traffic from a specific IP or website.

Redirect Non-WWW Traffic to WWW

You may notice that some websites can be accessed by typing the website URL with the WWW or without it. For example, both http://www.sitename.com and http://sitename.com point to the same website. While this is true, search engines still deal with both in a different ways and give both URLs different ranking. This is why you need to redirect the traffic from the non-WWW to the standard WWW URL. This is known as a *301 Redirect*, or *permanent redirect*. You can apply this 301 Redirect in the .htaccess file.

Redirect Non-WWW Traffic to WWW

1 In the .htaccess file, press **Enter** after the `RewriteEngine On` line.

2 Type **RewriteCond %{HTTP_HOST} !^www\.*sitename*\.com$**, replacing *sitename.com* with your website URL.

3 Press **Enter**.

4 Type **RewriteRule (.*)$ http://www.sitename/$1 [R=301,L].**

The new rules are added.

5 Click **File.**

6 Click **Save.**

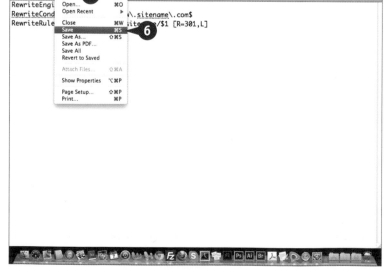

The Save As dialog box appears.

7 Navigate to the location where you want to save the file.

8 Type **.htaccess** in the Save As field, or in the File name field if you are using Microsoft Notepad.

9 Click **Save.**

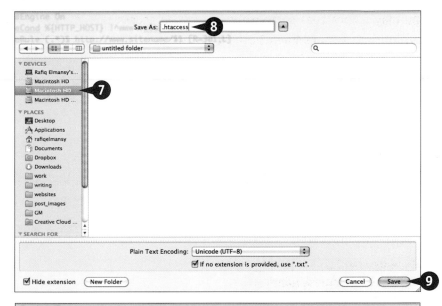

An alert message appears.

10 Click **Use ".".**

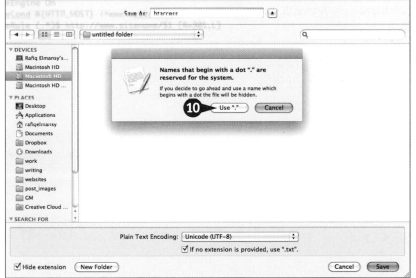

TIPS

What is the 301 Redirect's impact on SEO?
When you redirect your website traffic from a non-WWW URL to WWW URL, the web browsers and search engine crawlers redirect the traffic to the new URL. This can help you focus your SEO campaign on one URL and get more traffic and a higher ranking.

How do I figure out my website's indexing status?
You can check whether your website pages are indexed with or without the WWW. Go to www.google.com and type **Site:** *sitename.com* in the search field, replacing *sitename.com* with your website URL. Then, you can check whether the indexed page includes WWW.

Work with 301 Redirects

Websites are updated regularly and website pages may change based on updates. When a web page's location or name changes, search engines may not update this change and may still see the old name or path, which they interpret as website errors. In order to fix this, you need to manually use the 301 Redirect to redirect any traffic or search engine to the new web page's URL. It is also important to do this when you want to move the website from one domain to another without losing any traffic or affecting your ranking. You can apply the 301 Redirect from the .htaccess file.

Work with 301 Redirects

1 In the .htaccess file, press `Enter` after the `RewriteEngine On` line.

2 Type **Redirect 301 /oldwebpage. html http://www.sitename.com/ newwebpage.html**, replacing *oldwebpage.html* with your web page's old name, and replacing the *sitename.com/newwebpage. html* with the new web page URL.

3 Press `Enter`.

4 Type **RewriteRule (.*)$ http:// www.sitename/$1 [R=301,L]**. The new rules are added.

5 Click **File**.

6 Click **Save**.

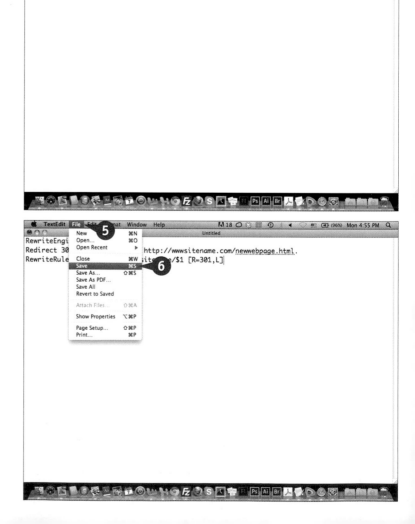

The Save As dialog box appears.

7 Navigate to the location where you want to save the file.

8 Type **.htaccess** in the Save As field, or in the File name field if you are using Microsoft Notepad.

9 Click **Save.**

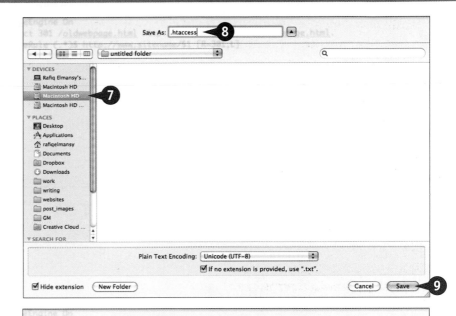

An alert message appears.

10 Click **Use ".".**

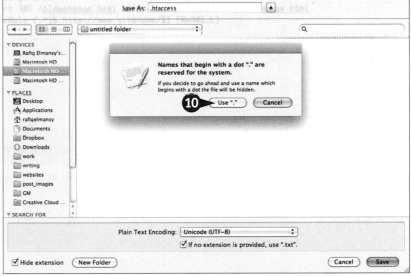

When do I use the 301 Redirect?

When you update your website, you have to consider the 301 Redirect to ensure that new web page links are updated in the different search engines and that no errors appear after you rename web pages or remove them from the server. Sometimes, it takes time to learn about the page errors for which these pages do not have replacements. In this case, you can simply redirect these pages to the website home page to avoid errors. If you own the .com, .net, or .org version of your URL, you can use the 301 Redirect to move all the traffic from these domains to the website's current active domain.

Scan Errors with W3C Markup Validation

When you build your website and update it, your code may include errors or it may not follow web standards. Although these errors are not obvious when you test your website, it is important to check for them and try to have as few of them as possible. Clean code that follows web standards helps the search engine spiders crawl your website quickly and index its pages more efficiently compared to code that is not compatible with the web standards. There are many ways you can check website code compatibility; one is the W3C Markup Validation website.

Scan Errors with W3C Markup Validation

① Type **http://validator.w3.org** in your web browser.

② Press **Enter**.

The W3C Markup Validation Service home page appears.

③ Type the website URL.

④ Click **More Options.**

The More Options section expands.

In this section, you can select options to run a more detailed check.

5 Click **Check.**

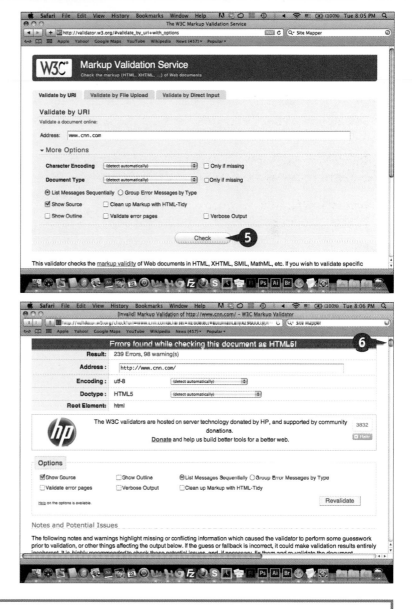

The website error results appear.

6 Scroll down to see the errors.

How do I fix website errors?
After you check the website and review the errors, you can click and choose the number of the lines to include for each result to display its place in the code. Then, you can go to the website code and fix the error to reduce the number of incompatibility issues on your website.

What is the validation icon?
When you check your website and get it validated, you can add the validation icon to your website. This icon shows that your website has a professional, validated code. You can use the code on this page to add the icon to your website http://validator.w3.org/docs/help.html#icon.

CHAPTER 4

Mastering Keywords

The term *keywords* in Search Engine Optimization (SEO) refers to the most important words or group of words in your website content. Keywords play an essential role in the SEO process because search crawlers use them to index your website. Thus, it is essential you understand how to leverage your website keywords for your SEO process to be a success.

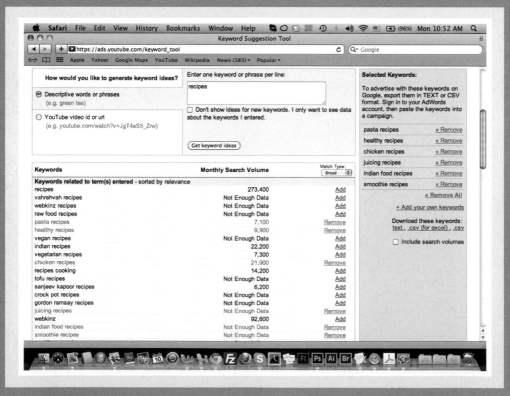

Understanding Keywords

Keywords are the most important part of SEO. Most SEO steps call for you to choose the keywords that best reflect your website's niche and to optimize your site either by optimizing the website content files for specific keyword, or by sending traffic and links to your website using these keywords. Therefore, it is essential you understand how to select website keywords and how to optimize them. Your website can focus on a number of keywords, and each page in your website should be optimized for a specific keyword to help the search engine display this page when users type this keyword in their search queries.

Select Website Keywords

Many factors affect which keywords you choose for your website. You must first determine the market niche and audience for your site. This helps you predict the search engine queries users will use. There are two types of websites with regard to keywords. The first type is websites that focus on a limited number of keywords or just one keyword. These websites are easy to optimize because you focus your SEO efforts on only one term. On the other hand, this limited keyword focus is very risky because you need to choose the best keyword; otherwise, it will not drive any traffic to your website. The second type is websites that include a number of different keyword categories. While these keywords are not related to each other, they are related to the same market niche. When you focus on these keywords in your website, it takes more effort during the SEO process to optimize content for each one.

Focus on Limited Number of Keywords

If you have a new website that you would like to optimize, you should focus on one category of keywords such as photography, wedding photography, photo effects, and nature photography. This will help your website to get indexed fast in the search engine and get ranked in these keywords better than the websites that do not focus on specific category keywords. Additionally, the SEO process for focused website are more easier than the websites that have wide range or keywords. When your website get ranked in specific keyword, you can move forward to focus on more keywords and so on.

Use Head Term Keywords

Head Terms refer to one- or two-word keywords such as "jobs," "fish food," and "mothers." These Head Terms keywords are very common and are used frequently to describe a website category or product. While these keywords require massive SEO efforts to optimize, they do not guarantee you will have success, especially when your website is new on the Internet. This is because search engines display older websites and products that include this keyword before displaying yours. For example, if you search for the word "Photoshop," you will notice that the first search results to appear are links from the product's company, along with websites such as Wikipedia and large technology news websites. Thus, it is wise to think in terms of long keywords instead of hard-to-reach Head Terms.

Use Long Tail Terms

Long Tail Terms refer to search keywords that include more than one word, such as "free online jobs," "fish types in the Red Sea," and "free tips for new mothers." Most users are trying to find specific information, so they do not type just one word in the query field and tend to include the important keywords in their search queries. Thus, the Long Tail Term keywords can be easier to target. While these keywords have fewer results than the Head Term keywords or the same search volume, your website has a better chance of appearing in search engines using Long Tail Term keywords. Building content that focuses on these keywords will help you improve your website traffic and rank over time.

Optimize Website Keywords

Keyword optimization is a slow, long-term process that requires time and effort in order to see a significant impact on your website. So, you have to focus on one keyword at a time, and once you finish optimizing some of your website content for this keyword, you can move on to another keyword. Keep in mind that you will get the best SEO results if you keep your keyword focus limited. If you are creating a new page on your website, you should use your keywords wisely, and focus each page on a specific keyword. For example, you can create an article for your website that talks about online business and include the keyword "online business tips" to get the page ranked for this keyword category.

Apply Keyword Optimization

There are different aspects to applying keyword optimization to a website. Your website's content is one of the most important parts to optimize because it is what the search engine displays when the user types a related keyword in the search query field. You also have to optimize the website links and menus to reflect website-focused keywords. For example, if your website niche is "online jobs search," you can have the menu links reflect this with text such as "Job search" and "Online jobs." The other part of the keyword optimization is the website code. You have to apply specific SEO methods to ensure that the website code is optimized for search engine indexing.

Analyze Keywords with SEMrush

To understand your website keywords, you need to use different tools to gather information about your website and the display analytics in your SEO campaign. SEMrush is a comprehensive tool that collects information about your website, your competitor's website, and the important keywords used on your website that bring effective traffic to it. The information that you get from SEMrush is gathered from both Google and Bing search engines. You can also find information about the links to your website and from where your traffic is coming.

Analyze Keywords with SEMrush

1 Type **www.semrush.com** in your web browser and press **Enter**.

The SEMrush page appears.

2 Click **Login** to sign in with your free account.

Note: You need to create a new account if you do not have an account.

The SEMrush login pop-up window appears.

3 Type your username.

4 Type your password.

5 Click **Login.**

The SEMrush dashboard appears.

6 Type **tripadvisor.com** in the search field.

7 Click **Search.**

TIPS

TIPS

Why is some information in SEMrush not available?
When you first register for SEMrush, you sign up for a free account where you can see a limited version of keyword search analytics. To see the rest of the analytics, you need to upgrade your free account. SEMrush prices range based on the number of results and other services that it provides. You can learn about their pricing at www.semrush.com/prices.html.

What are the different country-based results?
In the top of the search results, you can choose between different Google search results. For example, you can choose UK to display results from Google.co.uk. These options can give you more accurate analytics based on the search keywords used in each Google version.

continued ▶

Y ou can find more information about website search keywords in the Keyword Research menu on the SEMrush dashboard. Here you will find more data for the keywords, such as the search volume for each keyword, which refers to the number of searches that use it. You can find the cost of the keyword for advertisers and the number of search results returning the keyword. You can also learn about keywords related to the website search. This data can help you learn more about the most important keywords in your website, and how to use them in your SEO process.

Analyze Keywords with SEMrush (continued)

The search results appear.

8 Click the **Keyword Research** down arrow (▾).

The Keyword Research menu expands.

9 Click **Overview.**

The Keyword Research overview appears.

10 Scroll down to the Related keywords report.

More related keywords appear.

How do I find more information about website competitors?

Analyzing your competitors helps you learn about others in the same market, the keywords they use, and the techniques they apply to increase their traffic and rank. And analyzing your competitors' keywords gives you an idea about how they get their traffic and their position in Google's search results page. From the sidebar menu of SEMrush, you click the **Competitors** link under the Organic Research section. This shows you a list of different competitors, the competition level, common keywords, search engine keywords, search engine traffic, and the advertising keywords. You can always upgrade the account to get more results in the list and find more about the competency level.

Analyze Bing Search with SEMrush

In addition to showing keywords data from different Google websites, SEMrush can display data from the Bing search engine. This information includes keywords and competition from Bing visits, which can help you to learn about your website Bing statistics, as well as other websites, and learn how to optimize content for both the Bing and Google search engines. When you search for specific website keywords using the SEMrush search feature, you will have the option to choose to display data from either Google or Bing from the top-left buttons above the statistics section.

Analyze Bing Search with SEMrush

1 Type **tripadvisor.com** in the search field.

2 Click **Search.**

The search results appear.

3 Click **Bing** ( ).

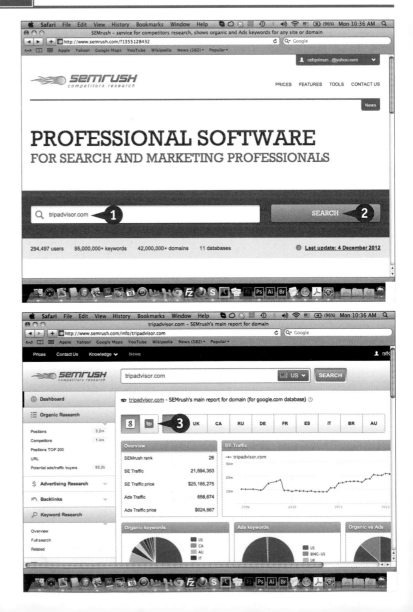

The Bing button becomes active.

④ Click **US.**

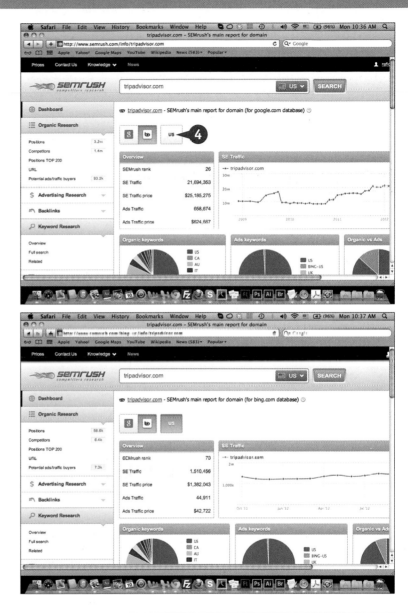

The dashboard displays information from the Bing search engine.

Why is it important to consider Bing in optimization?
Bing is one of the major search engines after Google. Currently, it collaborates with Yahoo search, which makes it good source for traffic to your website. For example, you can focus on the keywords that are shared by both the Google and Bing search engines. This can maximize the benefit of your keyword optimization in your website.

Can I share SEMrush data with others?
Yes, you can share the data you view in SEMrush with others through e-mail. On the top right of the dashboard, you can click the **Send by Email** icon to display a pop-up dialog box, where you can add your message and send it with a PDF version of the analytics.

Analyze Keywords with Keyword Discovery

Keyword Discovery is another method you can use to learn more about keywords and related Head Term and Long Tail Term keywords. Keyword Discovery provides both paid and free trial services, where you can display data related to each keyword. When you visit www.keyworddiscovery.com, you need to create an account and then start searching for the keyword that you would like to analyze. For example, you can search for "jobs" to get all the common search keywords related to the word "jobs." You can use this data to build website content related to jobs.

Analyze Keywords with Keyword Discovery

Analyze Keywords

1 Type **www.keyworddiscovery. com** in your web browser and press **Enter**.

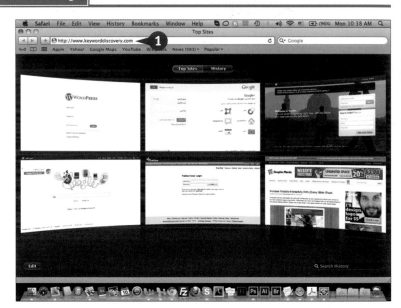

The Keyword Discovery page appears.

2 Click **Login** to sign in with your free account.

Note: You need to create a new account if you do not have an account.

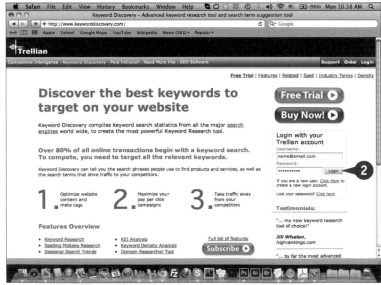

The Keyword Discovery home appears.

3 Type a search term.

4 Click the **Results per page** pop-up menu and select the number of results you want to appear per page.

5 Click the **Database** pop-up menu and select Global Premium from the database.

6 Click a specific search option category (□ changes to ☑).

7 Click **Search**.

The search query list appears.

TIP

What are the different search databases in Keyword Discovery?
When you do a keyword search, you can choose between different search databases, each with different results. For example, the Global Premium Database includes searches from different search engines, and these results are updated during the previous 12 months. The Historical Global Database returns search results since 2005 and includes results from 200 different sources. The Shopping Keywords Database includes keywords from different shopping websites, such as Buy.com, Bizrate.com, and Amazon.com. The eBay Keyword Database enables you to retrieve search keywords results from the eBay Partner Network. You can also search databases related to countries and specific search engines.

continued ▶ 75

Y ou can access many useful Keyword Discovery features from the menu. You can check keyword trends and find helpful tools under Keyword Tools. For example, the Keyword Density Tool helps you analyze a specific URL and learn about the different keywords in this URL. You can choose the search database and number of results to display per page. You can also customize options. For example, you can choose to display keywords with a minimum of two words in a phrase and a maximum of three words; avoid showing the Head Term keywords; and only display the Long Tail Term keywords.

Analyze Keywords with Keyword Discovery (continued)

Use the Keywords Density Tool

1 Position your mouse pointer over **Keyword Tools** to expand the menu.

2 Click **Keyword Density Tool.**

The Keyword Density Tool page appears.

3 Type the URL for which you would like to check its keywords.

4 Click the **Results** pop-up menu and select the number of research results you want to appear.

5 Click the **Select Database** pop-up menu and select a search engine; for example, Google.

6 Click the **Min. Keywords Per Phrase** pop-up menu and select the minimum number of keywords in the phrase to appear in a phrase.

7 Click the **Max. Keywords Per Phrase** pop-up menu and select the maximum number of keywords in the phrase to appear in a phrase.

8 Click **Search.**

The Keyword Density Tool
page results appear.

9 Click a keyword.

The search queries that are
related to this keyword
appears.

What is the Keyword Competitors Tool?

The Keyword Competitors Tool helps you analyze
your website competitors using the same keywords.
You can submit the keywords various ways, such as
uploading them as text files, extracting them from
HTML code tags, extracting them from specific
URLs, or simply writing them in the Keywords field.

What is the Keyword Trends Tool?

The Keyword Trends tool displays information about
a specific keyword such as the market share refers
to percentage of the keyword search volume in each
major search engine. When you type the keywords
in this tool and click **Search**, it returns information
about the keyword, including the search percentage
by country.

Compare Keywords with Yahoo Clues

Unlike the keyword tools, Yahoo Clues helps you analyze and compare trends using general keywords. When you compare two keywords from different trends or the same one, Yahoo Clues displays the percentage of female and male users, and their average ages. You can see a map with the countries searching for these keywords and their search percentages, as well as other related keywords. Yahoo Clues gives you a global overview of different trends, and then you can research them in greater depth. It does not require you to register or create an account to get the results.

Compare Keywords with Yahoo Clues

1 Type **http://clues.yahoo. com** in your web browser and press **Enter**.

The Yahoo Clues home page appears.

2 Click **Trend Analysis.**

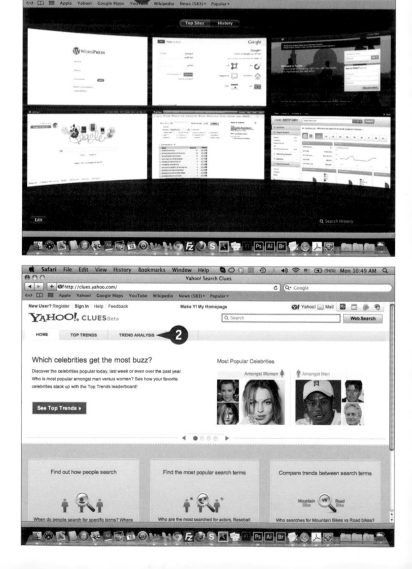

The Trend Analysis page appears.

③ Type a keyword in the first Find Trends field.

④ Type a keyword in the second Find Trends field.

⑤ Click a time period; for example, Month.

Ⓐ If you chose Month, click the **Number of months** arrows and select a specific number for comparison.

⑥ Click **Discover.**

The trends comparison results appear.

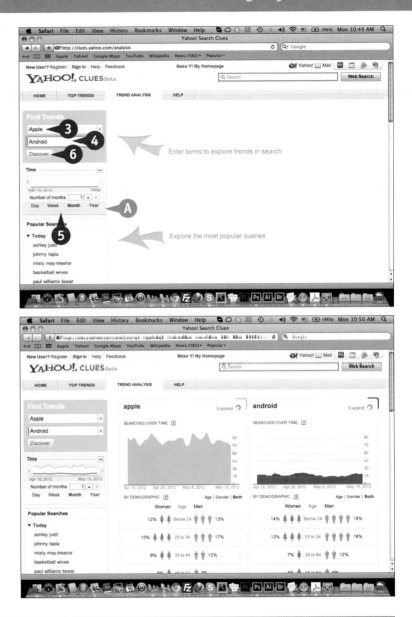

How do I switch between related trends in Yahoo Clues?
Yahoo Clues does not limit you to the currently submitted keywords and you can switch between different related keywords to view changes among them. In order to change the different keywords, you have to scroll down to the query section where the keywords are. Then, you can click any of the keywords from either section; notice that the comparison is updated with the new keyword and the new data appears. You can use this feature if you would like to compare related keywords from different trends. You can also set the comparison time range such as days, weeks, months, and years.

Work with the YouTube Keyword Tool

YouTube is a famous online video network. It provides a keyword tool to help YouTube video advertisers optimize their advertisements and video pages for search engines. This tool is helpful for giving you ideas about the search-related keywords. First, you need to choose the keyword language and country where you want to target your website or content. Then you add the keyword that you would like to search and YouTube returns related results.

Work with the YouTube Keyword Tool

1 Type **https://ads.youtube.com/keyword_tool** in your web browser and press **Enter**.

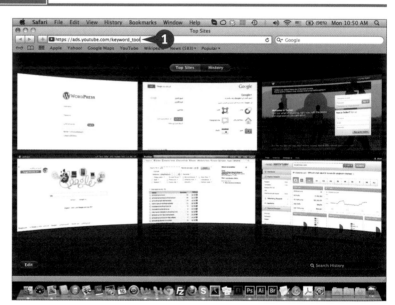

The YouTube Keyword Tool appears.

2 Select a language for your results; for example, English.

3 Select a country; for example, United States.

4 Type a keyword or phrase, noting one per line.

5 Click **Get keyword ideas.**

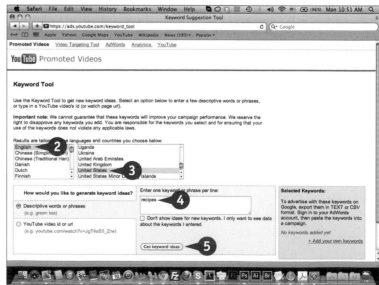

The keyword ideas list appears.

6 Click **Add** next to any keywords.

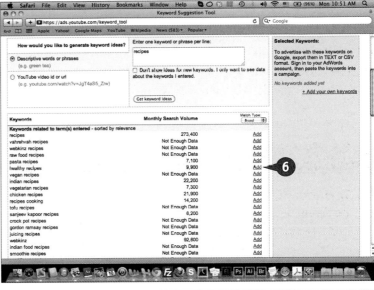

The keywords are added to the list on the right.

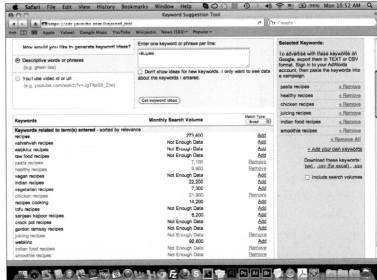

TIPS

How do I get keyword ideas from YouTube videos?

Instead of the keyword search, you can get keywords directly from a video URL. Just click the YouTube video ID or URL to switch to the video link field. In this field, add the video URL and click **Get keyword ideas** to display keywords related to the submitted video.

Can I download selected keywords to use with other tools?

Yes, you can download selected keywords from the list and use them with other tools. You can also add keywords that are not in the list to your custom keywords on the right side of the YouTube Keyword Tool. You can download the selected keywords in different formats, including TXT and CSV format for Microsoft Excel.

Analyze Your Website with Web SEO Analytics

Analytic tools are essential to SEO experts and site owners because they enable them to get data and information about a website's keywords and its position in search engine rankings. For example, you can focus your website SEO on a specific keyword to increase the website ranking for it. One company that provides comprehensive tools is Web SEO Analytics at www.webseoanalytics.com. Web SEO Analytics' free and premium tools enable you to test your website, analyze its keywords, and find more SEO information about its ranking and position on the search engine.

Analyze Your Website with Web SEO Analytics

1 Type **www.webseoanalytics. com** in your web browser and press Enter.

2 Click **SEO Tools.**

The free SEO tools page appears.

3 Click **Web SEO Analysis.**

The web SEO analysis page appears.

④ Type the website URL.

⑤ Click **Go.**

The website analysis data appears.

What is the Backlink Analysis tool?

Web SEO Analytics provides many tools, as you can see running down the left side of the screen, including the Backlink Analysis tool, which allows you to get information about the links that come to your website, which are known as *backlinks*. The more backlinks your website gets from high ranking websites, the higher the ranking it receives from Google. You can use this tool to analyze these backlinks and where they link on your website.

CHAPTER 5

Building On-Page SEO

The On-page search engine optimization (SEO) process includes the methods you apply to website pages and files to make them search engine optimized and apply to help search crawlers index them more efficiently, which in turn displays them in a higher position in the search result pages. Subsequently, these methods can increase your website's traffic and ranking in search engines.

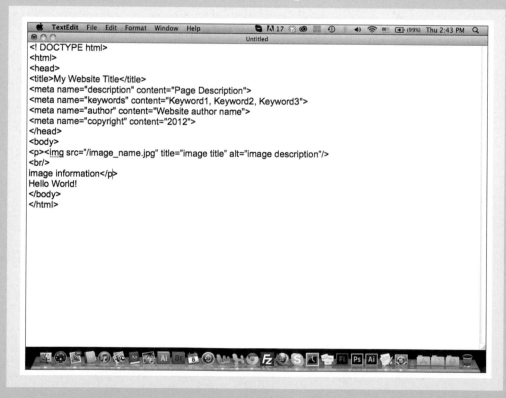

Build an HTML Document

On-page search engine optimization (SEO) techniques are applied to the code in web pages, filenames, and content. To apply On-page optimization, you need to have a basic understanding of HTML (Hypertext Markup Language), which is the programming language used to create web pages. HTML uses commands called *tags* to tell the browser how to display content. For example, you need to add *Meta tags* to the <head> tags in HTML documents. These Metadata tags provide information to search engines about your page. You can start building HTML documents using text editors such as TextEdit for the Mac and Notepad for Windows.

Build an HTML Document

1 Click the **Finder** icon ( ).

Note: For Windows users, you can click **Start,** click **All Programs,** click **Accessories,** and then click **Notepad.**

The Finder window opens.

2 Click **Applications.**

The installed applications appear.

3 Click **TextEdit.app.**

The text editor opens.

4 Type **<! DOCTYPE html>** to define the document as an HTML file.

5 Press Enter.

6 Type the opening **<html>** tag to open all the HTML files.

7 Press Enter

8 Type the opening **<head>** tag.

9 Press Enter.

10 Type **</head>** to close the **<head>** tag.

11 Press Enter.

12 Type the opening **<body>** tag.

13 Press Enter.

14 Type the text **Hello World!.**

15 Press Enter.

16 Type the closing **</body>** tag.

17 Press Enter.

18 Type the closing **</html>** to indicate the end of the HTML document.

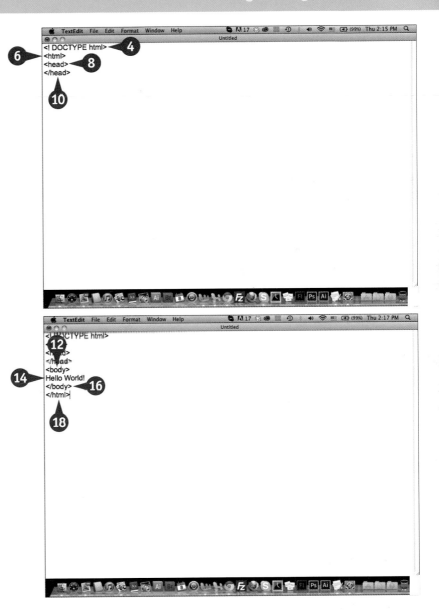

Can I use a text editor to view existing HTML code?
Yes, you can view the codes for existing HTML documents by simply opening them in your text editor application. When you open an HTML document, you see the code in the browser by right-clicking the page and clicking **View Source.** Viewing the code for existing web pages shows you how code should flow and how SEO techniques have been applied.

What are the WYSIWYG HTML editors?
WYSIWYG is an acronym for *What You See Is What You Get*. It describes HTML editors that allow you to use commands and icons to build web pages without having to write the code manually.

Add a Page Title Meta Tag

*T*itle is the most important meta tag and appears at the top of your web page code, directly after the <head> tag. Search crawlers index the Title meta tag and display it in the search results. You can view a website's Title meta tag by opening the website in the web browser; the title appears at the top of the browser or tab. Thus, the title should be descriptive of the page's content and include the important optimized keywords. The title should be less than 70 characters; otherwise Google will omit the extra characters from the search results.

Add a Page Title Meta Tag

1 Click after the end of the <head> tag.

2 Press **Enter**.

3 Type the opening **<title>** tag.

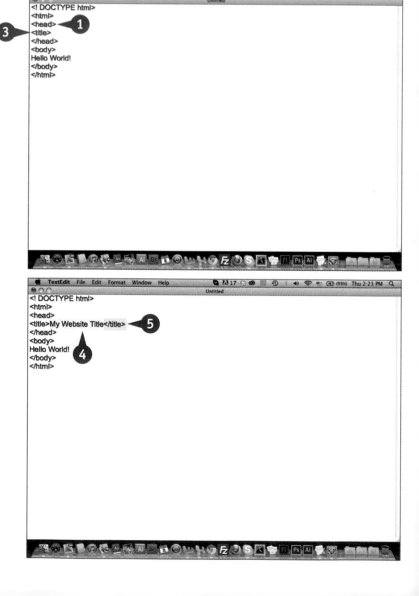

4 Type the text **My Website Title.**

5 Type the closing **</title>** tag.

Add a Page Description Meta Tag

Description is another meta tag that you add at the top of the web page, inside the <head> tag. The Description meta tag provides a brief summary of the webpage and its content. Search crawlers use this tag to get information about the page content and display it in the search results. Unlike with the Title tag, you can use a greater number of characters to describe your website. The character limit for the site description is 155 characters. Make sure to use optimized keywords that represent the website content.

Add a Page Description Meta Tag

1 Click after the end of the </title> tag.

2 Press **Enter**.

3 Type **<meta name="description"**.

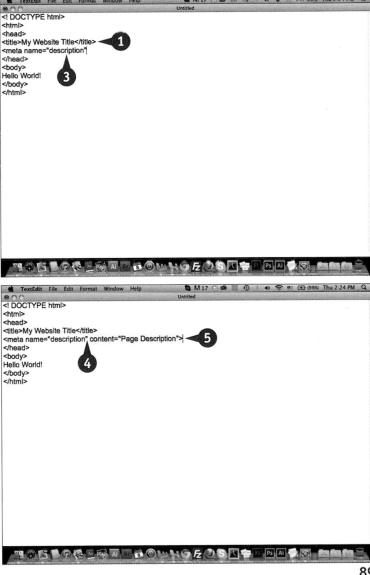

4 Press **Spacebar**.

5 Type **content="*Page Description"***>, replacing *Page Description* with your website description.

Add a Page Keyword Meta Tag

The *Keyword* meta tag includes individual keywords separated by commas. Similar to the description and title tags, the search engine crawlers use the Keyword meta tag information to index the website and display it in the search results. The keywords should be descriptive and optimized to ensure that the search engine displays the website when users search for these specific keywords. Limit your number of keywords to around 2 to 5 percent of your content. Overloading your web page with keywords is considered *stuffing*, and it may negatively affect your Google rank. Some search engines overlook the Keyword tag, but it is still useful in others.

Add a Page Keyword Meta Tag

1 Click after the Description meta tag.

2 Press **Enter**.

3 Type **<meta name="keywords"**.

4 Press **Spacebar**.

5 Type **content="***Keyword1, Keyword2, Keyword3***">**, replacing *Keyword1, Keyword2, and Keyword3* with your website optimized keywords.

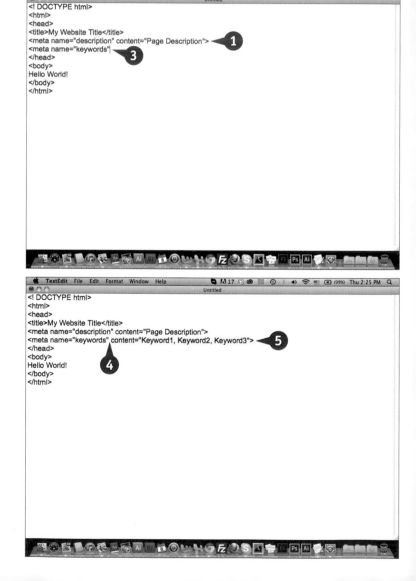

Add Author and Copyright Meta Tags

The *Author* and *Copyright* meta tags are optional and are not as important as the Title, Description, and Keyword meta tags. However, they do make your web page look professional. The Author meta tag includes information about the web page's creator, or webmaster, as well as contact information, an e-mail, and the company name. The Copyright meta tag defines website copyrights and ownership. You can use it to include information such as a trademarked name.

Add Author and Copyright Meta Tags

Add the Author Meta Tag

1 Click after the Keywords meta tag.

2 Press Enter.

3 Type **<meta name="author"**.

4 Press Spacebar.

5 Type **content="*Website author name*">**, replacing *Website author name* with your website-optimized keywords.

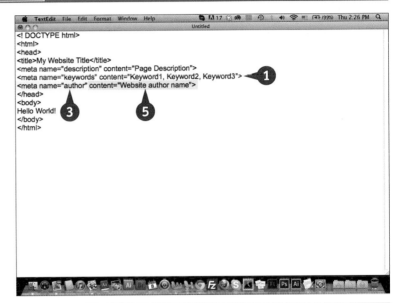

Add the Copyright Meta Tag

6 Click after the Author meta tag.

7 Press Enter.

8 Type **<meta name="copyright"**.

9 Press Spacebar.

10 Type **content="*2012*">**, replacing *2012* with your website copyright information.

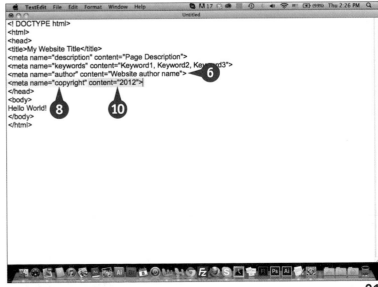

Save an HTML Document

You can save the HTML code that you write in any text editor or HTML editor using an .html or .htm format. Both formats are web browser compatible. The way you name the HTML document is important in SEO. The name should be descriptive, short, and represent the website structure. For example, you can name the contact page Contactus.html. The main web page is usually named index.html or default.html. When you create your web page names, use only letters, numbers, hyphens (-), periods (.), and underscores (_). Also, make sure to avoid using spaces or special characters in the filename.

Save an HTML Document

1 Click **File** in the TextEdit application.

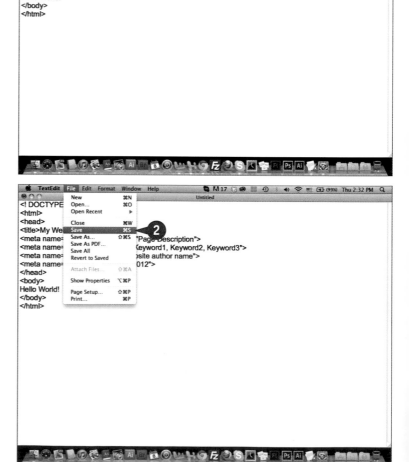

The File menu opens.

2 Click **Save.**

The Save As dialog box appears.

③ Navigate to the location where you want to save the file.

④ Type the name of the file, **index.html**, in the Save As field.

⑤ Click **Save**.

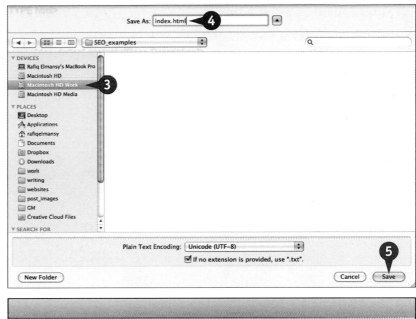

An alert message appears.

⑥ Click **Use .html** to save your document as an HTML file.

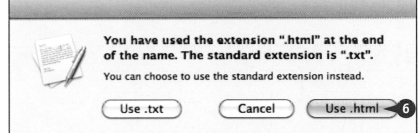

You have used the extension ".html" at the end of the name. The standard extension is ".txt".

You can choose to use the standard extension instead.

Use .txt   Cancel   Use .html ⑥

TIPS

What makes the HTML code search engine optimized?

When the search engine crawlers crawl websites, they read the HTML source code for every web page on the website. So, it is important to keep your code clear and organized. For example, you need to make sure to add the meta tags at the top of the website and avoid using complex codes and unwanted tags.

What is the different between .html and .htm?

In the early Windows versions, the file extensions were limited to three characters, making .htm the default extension for HTML files. Nowadays, this limitation no longer exists. There are still some applications that use .htm as the default format for HTML documents, .html has become universal and is recommended.

Optimize Image Filenames and Alt Attributes

Images should be optimized for the search engines. While the search engine crawlers do not see the images, they can crawl the image tag (`<img>`) in the HTML code. The image filenames should reflect the image content. The `alt` attribute is an image tag value that describes the image for the search engine. The `caption` attribute appears under the images and describes them for the search engine as well. `title` is another image tag attribute. While it is not mandatory in SEO, it is still important to build a professional image tag in your HTML code.

Optimize Image Filenames and Alt Attributes

Add the Image File

1 Click after the `<body>` tag.

2 Press **Enter**.

3 Type **`<p><img src="/image_name.jpg" />`**, replacing the *image_name.jpg* with your image filename.

Note: The previous steps upload the images to the website's root folder. See the Tips section for more details.

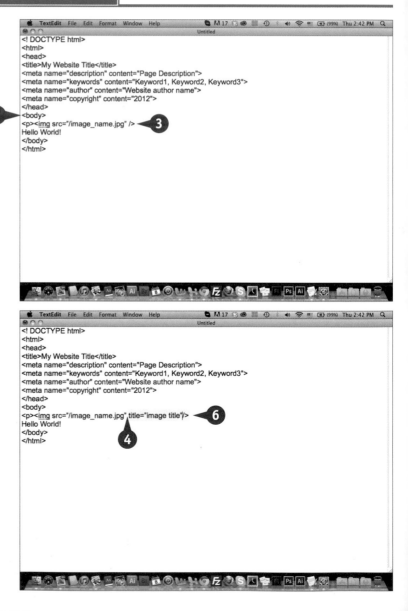

Add the Image Title Attribute

4 Click after `<p><img src="/image_name.jpg"`.

5 Press **Spacebar**.

6 Type **`title="image title"`**, replacing *image title* with your image's title name.

Add the Image Alt Attribute

7 Click after `title="image title"`.

8 Press **Spacebar**.

9 Type **alt=_"image description"_**, replacing _image title_ with description text for your image.

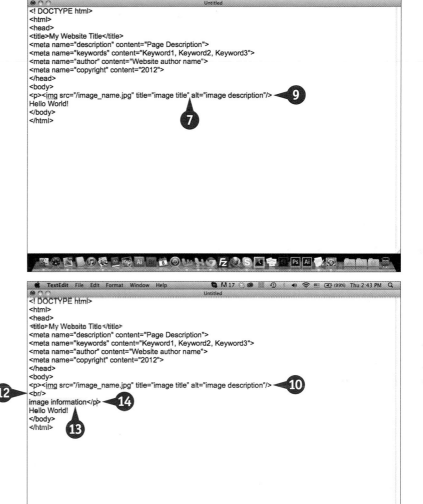

Add the Image Caption

10 Click after the `alt="image description"/>`.

11 Press **Enter**.

12 Type **
** to create a new line on the web page.

13 Type **_image information_**, replacing _image information_ with information text about the image.

14 Type the paragraph closing tag **</p>**.

How do I upload images to the server?

You upload images to the website server using _FTP (File Transfer Protocol)_. It allows you to upload images and files to a server and display them by typing the server's URL or image path in your browser.

What are the best image formats to use?

Web browsers support various formats, such as JPG, PNG, and GIF. JPG is the most commonly used format. It maintains good quality, and the file size is smaller. PNG is suitable for images that include transparent parts. The images are good quality; however, the file sizes are larger than JPGs. GIF supports both still image and animated sequence. It has a low color range support of only 256 colors.

Optimize Your Website Content

The search engine crawls your website for the content mainly to retrieve the information users are looking for when they type a search keyword in the search field. Therefore, your website content should be optimized to ensure optimal engine indexing. Optimizing website content is twofold. First you optimize the content itself using keyword density, content formatting, and the content itself. Second you optimize the HTML and CSS (Cascading Style Sheets) code that you use to format the content display. The content loading speed is another important factor to consider.

Develop CSS and HTML Clean Code

When you develop the webpage HTML and CSS, you have to consider that the search engine will crawl this code. Therefore, it should be well organized and clean, so the crawler can easily index your web page content without encountering any errors that would affect the indexing process. You can check for website errors using website validation service sites such as http://validator.w3.org. You can use this website to check your web page for errors, and then return to the code and fix them.

Improve the Content Loading Time

One of the important steps in the SEO process is the web page content loading time. Fast-loading websites let users access content more easily and faster than slow loading websites. Additionally, the crawlers will be able to crawl more pages from your website in a shorter time and index them faster. Optimizing the loading time includes using small image file sizes, avoiding code complexities, and implementing JavaScript. You can check your website's loading time using http://tools.pingdom.com/fpt.

Set Keyword Density

The search engine determines the relativity of the content through keywords within the content. If your content includes the right density of keywords, that is the percent of times your keyword appears on a page relative to all the words on a page, the content has a greater chance of displaying in the search engine pages when a user types related search keywords in the search engine's search field. The placement of the keywords should be natural and not affect the quality of the content. The

optimal keyword density varies, but generally 2 to 5 percent is a good range. It is important to check the keyword density for each of your website pages. This helps you identify how well the content is optimized for search engines. You can use many tools to check the density of a specific keyword on your website page; one example is www.gorank.com/analyze.php.

Use Internal Links

Internal links refer to the links on your web page and links to other relative content within the same website. For example, you can use a keyword in an article as a link to a related article on the same website. These links are very important because the greater the number of internal links you have, the higher your website rank. The internal links play an important role in increasing page views because website visitors click internal links to view other pages on the website. Also, you can add internal links

to a web page by mentioning related topics. There are different web tools that help you check the internal links, such as www.google.com/webmasters/tools and www.seochat.com/seo-tools/site-link-analyzer. Unlike the Google Webmaster Tools, SEO Chat lets you check website internal links without creating a website account.

CHAPTER 6

Building Off-Page SEO

Off-page SEO is the optimization process that you perform to increase your website's popularity, rank, and traffic. Link building includes a number of steps you take to help increase the high-quality external links that link back to your website's main domain or internal posts; using keywords known as *anchor text* is one.

Find the Domain History

Before you start to create your Off-page campaign, you need to understand the market for your website niche and the other related websites within the same category. Because the link-building process depends on the relativity of the link that points to your website, the first step is to check the partner website's history and other information. It gives you an idea of when the website was established or the website age. Older websites have better reputations on Google than newer websites because Google considers them trusted websites and, subsequently, has confidence in their links.

Find the Domain History

1 Type **www.domaintools.com** in your web browser and press **Enter**.

The Domain Tools website appears.

2 Type the URL in the field.

3 Click **Search for Domain.**

The domain information appears.

④ Click **Registration**.

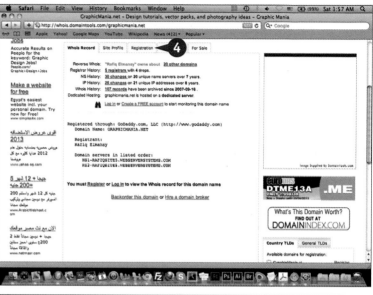

The domain history information appears.

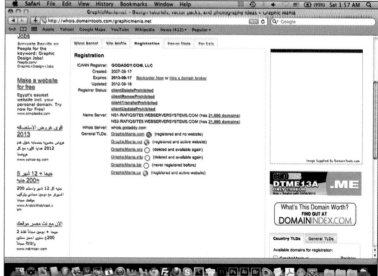

TIPS

What is the Site Profile tab?
The Site Profile tab includes information about a website so you have a better idea about its category and focus. It retrieves this data from the website's HTML code, called *Metadata*, and displays it so you can understand its relativity to your own website.

What is the website's Server Stats?
It is important to learn about the server that hosts the website that you are searching for, because it helps you to determine if the website is reliable and whether your links on this server will have a good reputation with Google indexing. You can learn about the website's server from the information under the Server Stats and the Who is Record tabs, which show the type of server hosting the website.

Review Website Backlinks

The backlinks are links that appear on other sites on the Internet. These backlinks can link to your website home page or inner pages. These backlinks are very important in the SEO process, because the more links you have, the higher amount of traffic your website receives, which increases its rank. You can obtain backlinks by using guest posts, buying text links, submitting website to directories, submitting press releases, and so on. Backlinks from related and other high-ranking websites that link to your website can help increase your website's rank in search engines faster.

Review Website Backlinks

1 Type **www.google.com** in your web browser and press **Enter**.

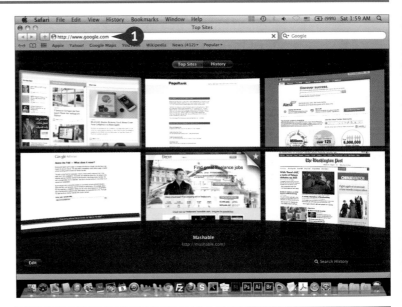

The Google search page appears.

2 Type **link: _http://www. mashable.com**, replacing the website link with your own website, and press **Enter**.

The links for the website appear.

③ Hover over the result to see a preview.

④ Scroll down the page.

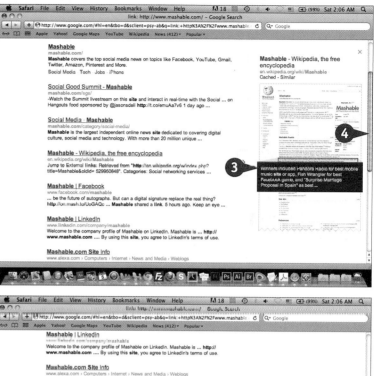

The end of the page appears.

④ You can click the navigation arrow to show more results.

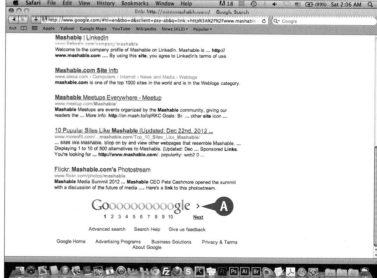

TIP

What are the internal and external links?

The website backlinks consist of two types. The *internal links* are linked words within the website itself and link to other pages on the same site. They can be used to guide the reader to more information on a specific topic or related topic. They are also helpful for increasing the page views for the website because users will navigate more pages, which increases the time they remain on your website. The *external links* refer to links to your website home page or internal pages from other websites. These websites provide links to yours to provide helpful or related information to their readers.

Gather Website Information

Website information is the most important for the SEO expert. Without the information, you cannot build an optimization plan. The Open Site Explorer (www.opensiteexplorer.org) is a comprehensive tool that allows you to learn about your website in more detail. It shows your website's authority, which reflects its ranking potential in different search engines, the links to the main domain or home page, and the total links to the website's pages. If you upgrade to a paid account, you can learn more about the website's social network information, such as its links on Facebook, Twitter, and Google +.

Gather Website Information

1 Type **www.opensiteexplorer.org** in your web browser and press **Enter**.

The Open Site Explorer appears.

2 Type a website domain name.

3 Click **Search.**

The website's information
appears.

4 Click **Anchor Text.**

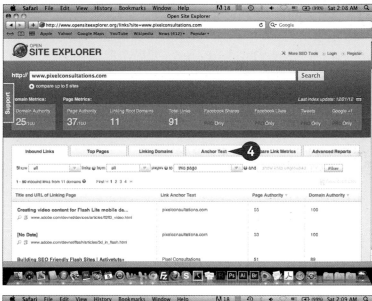

A A list of the keywords that
link to your website appears.

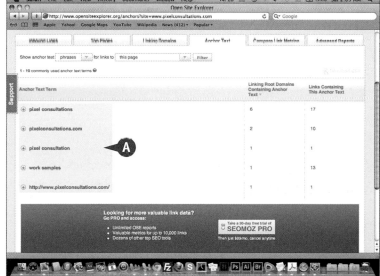

What are inbound and outbound links?
Inbound refers to links that link to your website
from other sites, while *outbound* refers to links that
go from your website to external websites. For
example, the Inbound Links tab in Open Site
Explorer shows links to your website, text used in
the links, and the original websites' authority. You
can learn more under the Linking Domains tab.

How do I compare statics for two websites?
You can compare statics for two or more sites under
the Compare Link Metrics tab. Click **+ Add URL** to
add up to four websites and compare them with
your initial site. The comparison shows the sites'
authority, internal and external links, and types
of links.

Compare Traffic for Websites

Alexa rank is one of the important indicators for comparing your website traffic with other sites in the same niche on the web. Alexa rank gives an estimate for a website's popularity and you can use it as an indicator for your website's traffic value. You can use Alexa for comparing other sites' traffic ranking to yours, and apply this information to your link building plans, such as deciding whether to partner with these websites or just analyze their performance. Alexa allows you to compare up to four websites to the main website and get the comparison details as Graphs on the chart.

Compare Traffic for Websites

1 Type **www.alexa.com** in your web browser and press **Enter**.

2 Type the website link.

3 Click **Search** (🔍).

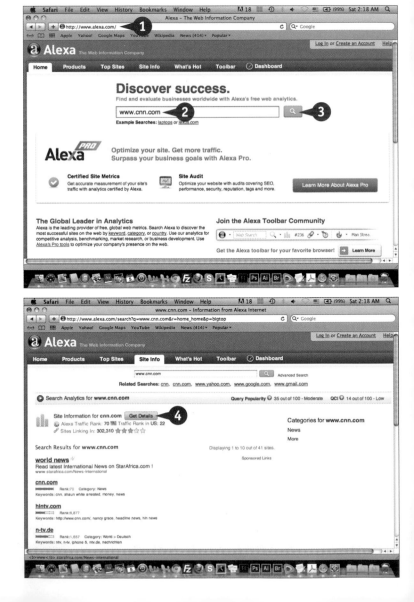

The website's Alexa rank appears.

4 Click **Get Details.**

The website details appear.

5 Type the website you would like to compare.

6 Click **Compare.**

A The comparison appears on the graph.

TIPS

What other information can I learn from Alexa?

Alexa lets you learn about the website page views, the amount of time users stay on the website, the audience demographics, and the Clickstream, which shows traffic sources and where users go after leaving the website. It also shows related websites and the percentage of traffic by country.

What is the Alexa toolbar?

Alexa provides a toolbar that you can install on your browser, and it helps you view statistics for a website in your browser rather than having to search for it on the Alexa website. You can also create a toolbar and customize it at www.alexa. com/toolbar-creator.

Check a Link Partner's Page Rank

Google assigns a *Page Rank* (PR) for every website on the Internet, which ranges from 0 to 10 based on a website's backlink reputation. Getting links from these websites to yours copies this rank to your website and helps it receive a higher rank. You need to get a lot of links from medium rank PR websites to get the same results as you get from high rank PR websites. You can check the PR for the websites that you want to get links from using Page Rank checkers such as www.prchecker.info.

Check a Link Partner's Page Rank

1 Type **www.prchecker.info** in your web browser and press `Enter`.

The Page Rank page appears.

2 Type the website you would like to check.

3 Click **Check PR.**

The verification page appears.

4 Type the number and letter combination shown on the verification image.

5 Click **Verify Now.**

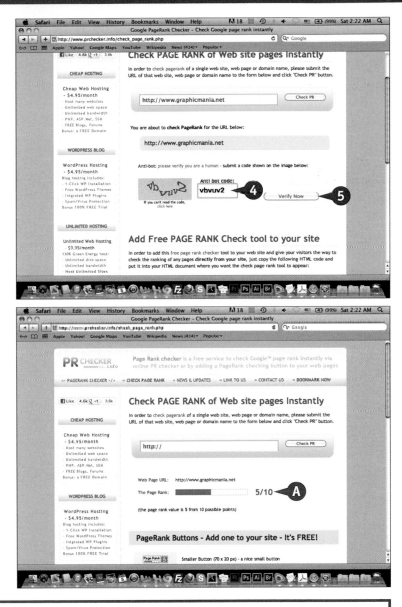

A The website's Page Rank appears.

TIPS

What are Google Page Rank updates?

On a regular basis, Google makes changes in its search algorithm to enhance the search process and update the Page Rank for different websites. These updates are known as Google Panda and Penguin updates, and can affect your website and other sites in one way or another. You can learn about the history of different changes in the Google algorithm at www.seomoz.org/google-algorithm-change.

What is Google Dance?

When Google applies Page Rank updates, you can find they fluctuate for some time until they become stable; this process is known as *Google Dance*, and it happens because updating data on different Google servers around the world takes some time.

Submit Your Website to a Link Directory

Ohe of the initial steps in building links to your website is submitting your website to a link directory, which organizes different websites based on category and niche. Some of these directories are free and others offer paid subscriptions. When you submit your website, you have to make sure that the link directory has a high Page Rank. Two of the most important directories are the Yahoo Directory at http://dir.yahoo.com, which charges a fee; and Dmoz at www.dmoz.org, which allows you to submit your website for free.

Submit Your Website to a Link Directory

1 Type **www.dmoz.org** in your web browser and press **Enter**.

The Dmoz home page appears.

2 Click a topic to start navigating to a terminal category.

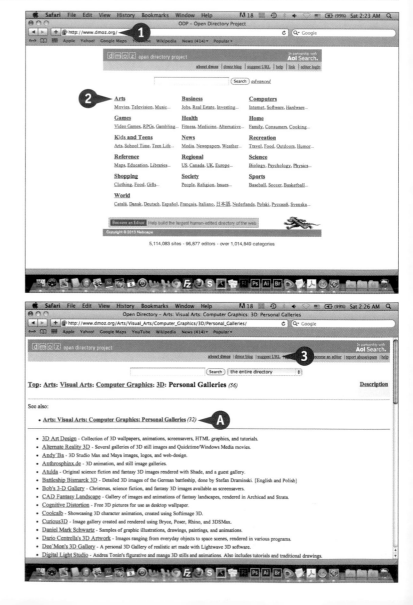

A The subcategory page appears.

3 Click **Suggest URL.**

The Submission form appears.

4 Complete the form, scrolling down as you go.

5 Scroll down to the end of the page.

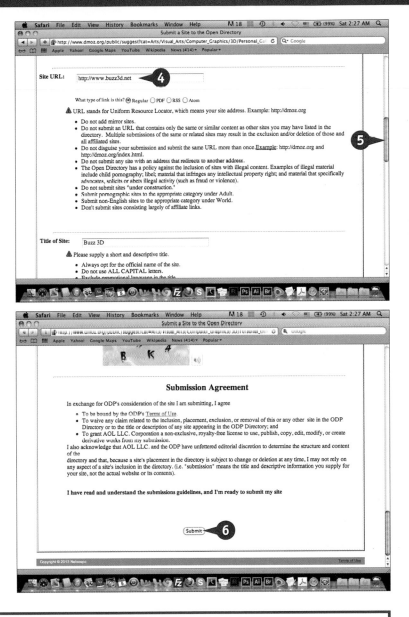

The end of the form appears.

6 Click **Submit.**

The website is submitted to Dmoz for review. It can take few months to list your approved website.

How long does it take to be listed in the Dmoz directory?
Dmoz can take a long time to accept your website and display it in their directory. Therefore, you have to be careful when submitting your website; you need to have it in good shape to avoid being rejected. Also, you need to submit it to the proper category and complete the form with accurate information about the website.

What are some other useful directories?
You can visit www.directorycritic.com for lists of directories where you can submit your website and the Page Rank for each directory. You can also view directories based on their payment model.

Submit to the Article Directories

Article directories include article archives from different fields and interests. Users submit their articles, creating an information source that others can use or find in search engine results. You can increase your website traffic and backlinks by writing guest articles for these websites and including links back to your website for the related keywords. There are many article directories on the web, and the most famous one is Ezine at http://ezinearticles.com.

Submit to the Article Directories

1 Type **http://ezinearticles.com** in your your web browser and press **Enter**.

Note: If you do not have an account, you can create one by clicking **Join.**

The Ezine website appears.

2 Click **Sign in.**

The Sign In page appears.

3 Type your e-mail address.

4 Type your password.

5 Click **Sign In**.

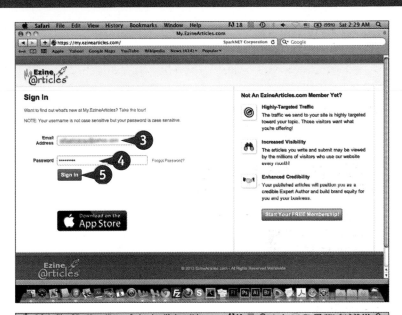

The home page appears.

6 Click **Submit an Article.**

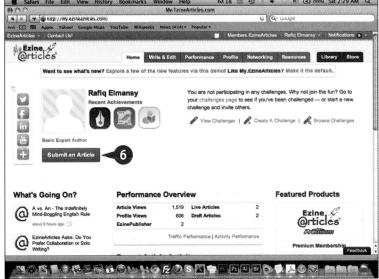

What type of links do the directories provide?
The article directories provide one-way links to your website or web page. A *one-way* link refers to a link to a website without a link back to the original linked page. This type of link ensures a better ranking than *two-way* links.

What other article directories are available?
While Ezine is the most popular article directory, there are other article directories where you can submit articles, such as GoArticles at http://goarticles.com, Article Dashboard at www.article dashboard.com, and Galoor at www.galoor.com.

continued ▶

Submit to the Article Directories (continued)

When you add your article to Ezine, it provides real-time guidance so you can make sure that your article follows the basic rules; this ensures it is well-optimized and does not include excessive promotions. You can fix any issues in your article by following the alert messages. At the end of the article submission forms, there is a resource area where you can promote your links that are related to the article topic.

Submit to the Article Directories (continued)

The Submit New Article form appears.

7 Click the **Title** area.

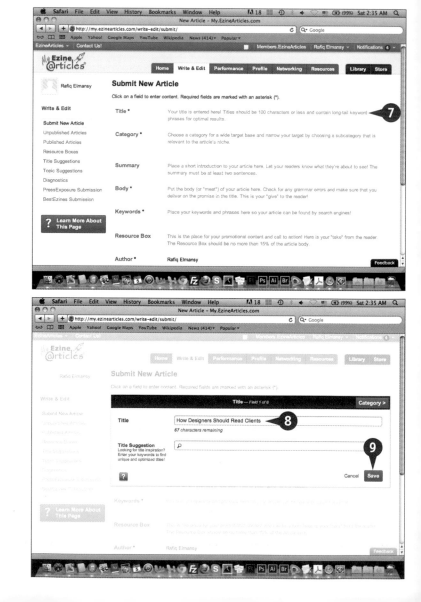

The Title pop-up message appears.

8 Type the article title.

9 Click **Save.**

The New Article form reappears.

10 Continue completing the remaining fields.

11 Click **Submit This Article.**

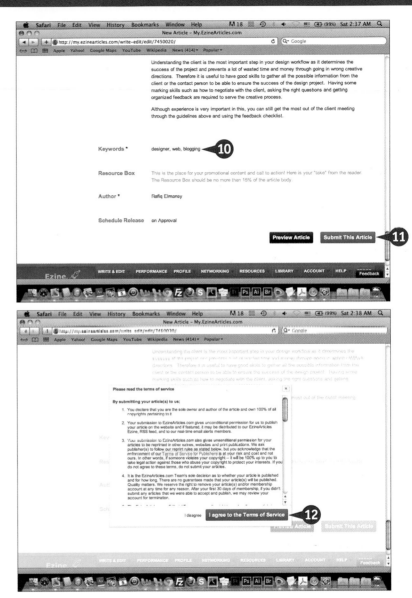

The Terms of Service message box appears.

12 Click the **I agree to the Terms of Service** option.

After the article is approved, it will publish to the Ezine website.

TIP

How do I get professional articles?

Writing articles is a talent that some people do not have. However, it is important to provide professional articles that attract users to read them and click the links in them. You can use professional article writing services, where you provide the topic of the article and a professional writer writes it for you. One of these services is MediaPiston at www.mediapiston.com. It provides various types of articles, ranging in price. There is also Godot at www.godotmedia.com.

Get Paid Backlinks

While you can acquire backlinks to your website naturally by getting other sites to link to your website, you can also get backlinks by buying links to your website from related sites in the market. These paid backlinks can occur when users link directly to your website or when they link to specific keywords in an article, which takes them to your website. The second type provides more natural backlinks because they come from related keywords from sites in the same niche as your website. One paid link provider is Text Link Ads at www.text-link-ads.com.

Get Paid Backlinks

1 Type **www.text-link-ads.com** in your web browser and press **Enter**.

2 Click **Login**.

Note: If you do not have an account, click Register to create an account.

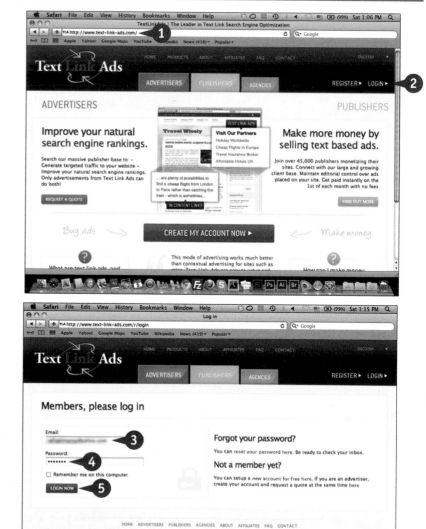

The login page appears.

3 Type your e-mail address.

4 Type your password.

5 Click **Login Now**.

The Advertiser Dashboard page appears.

6 Click **Text Link Ads.**

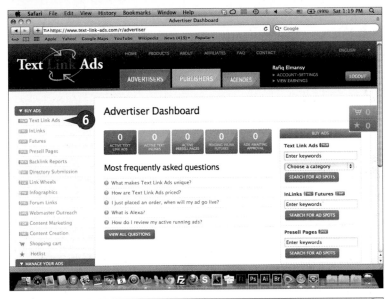

The Ad Search & Filter page appears.

7 Type the keyword that you used as a link.

8 Click **Search For Ad Spots.**

Locate the website on which you would like to advertise.

9 Click the **Add to Cart** button.

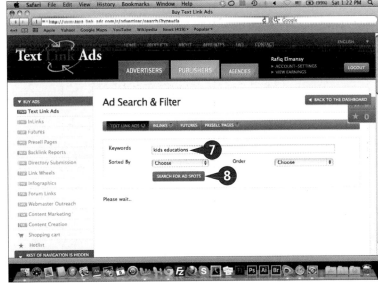

TIPS

Do paid links conflict with Google policies?

Google does not recommend paid links or buying backlinks. However, not all paid links are bad, especially ones that appear natural from related websites and from high-ranked websites. These links can influence the Google algorithm positively. So, you need to avoid links from advertisers that place links in unrelated links.

How do I get backlinks directly from related websites?

Besides buying the links from link networks, such as www.linkworth.com and www.textlinkbrokers. com, you can search for websites in your niche and contact them directly to either purchase paid links or exchange links with them.

Write Guest Posts

One method for getting backlinks is to write guest posts on other websites in the same category as yours. When you write guest post articles, you include links back to your website content in the article's resources and related topics. This type of back linking is natural and can help your website get a better ranking though the increasing number of related links. One guest post website is www.payperpost.com. Here you can describe the type of posts you need and your site's target to get offers from other writers and bloggers.

Write Guest Posts

1 Type **www.payperpost.com** in your web browser and press **Enter**.

2 Click **Login** to display the login message.

3 Type your e-mail address.

4 Type your password.

5 Click **Login** again.

Note: If you do not have an account, you can create one as an advertiser.

The Create new opportunity page appears.

6 Type the name of the opportunity.

7 Click **create opp**.

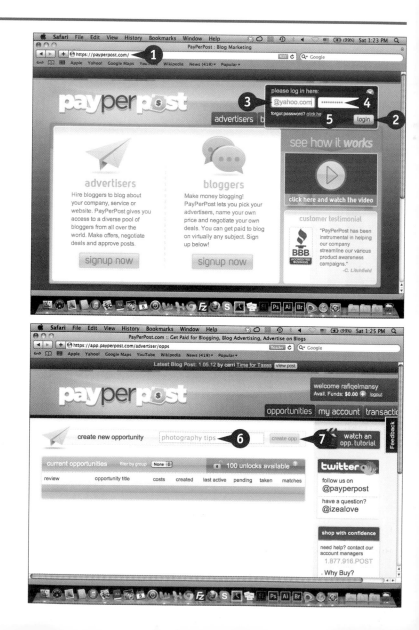

The creating opp (opportunity) dialog box appears.

8 Click the **step 1** to **step 4** tabs to complete the guest post requirements.

9 Click **next.**

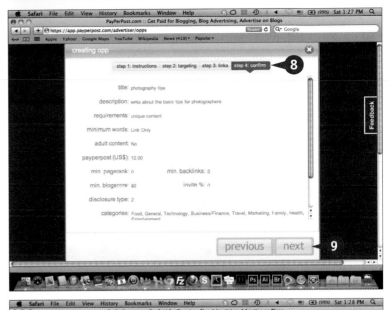

The terms of service page appears.

10 If your opportunity contains adult content, click this option (☐ changes to ☑).

11 Click **I agree.**

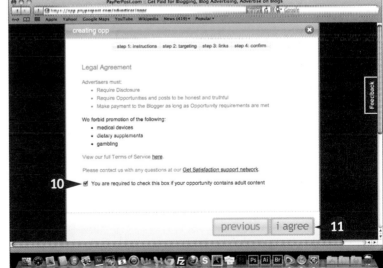

How do I add links in the Pay Per Post guest posts?
You can add up to three different links in one pay-per-post article. These links ensure the quality of the article and do not conflict with any Google regulations. You can add three links in the opportunity links list, and then choose to add one link randomly or all three links to your article.

How do I use guest posts for link building?
After writing the guest post, you can contact the websites in your niche and ask them to publish your guest posts. Some websites publish your guest post for free and others charge a fee.

Submit Press Releases

Press releases are one of the efficient methods for building backlinks and distributing them among different news sites, news grabbers, and search engines. A press release can include updates from your website or news service that you include on your website. These releases include information about your website and link to the updated content. A successful press release should be well written and submitted to a good press release website. There are many press release websites that provide free submission, such as www.free-press-release.com.

Submit Press Releases

1 Type **www.free-press-release.com** in your web browser and press **Enter**.

2 Click **Login**.

Note: If you do not have an account, click **Create Free Account** to create an account.

The Login Account page appears.

3 Type your e-mail address.

4 Type your password.

5 Click **Sign in.**

The Submit Press Release page appears.

6 Click **Submit Free PR.**

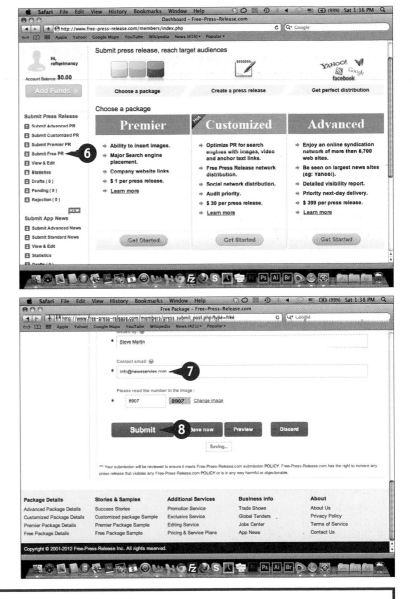

A new press release page appears.

7 Complete the form.

8 Click **Submit.**

The news is submitted for publishing on the Free Press Release website.

What is the different between free and a paid press release?

While a free press release provides basic benefits, a paid press release includes more and ensures that the press release appears on the high-traffic websites and search engines' news, such as the news on Yahoo, Bing, and Google. It also allows you to distribute your press release among large websites and their followers. The cost to submit a press release ranges from free submission to $400 or more in the United States. As a start, use the free services to get practice writing press releases and to see their initial impact on your website. There are different free press release providers, such as www.prweb.com, www.prnewswire. com, and www.24-7pressrelease.com.

Submit Your Site to Link Exchange

A *link exchange* is the process of two or more sites exchanging links. The exchanged links can be added to all the site's pages, which is known as *site wide*; or to only specific pages. You can do a link exchange with sites in your niche by directly contacting the site's owner and exchanging links. You add the owner's link code to your website and vice versa, or you can register your website with link-exchange websites such as Link Market at www.linkmarket.net. With this website, you submit your website and exchange links with other sites in the Link Market directory.

Submit Your Site to Link Exchange

① Type **www.linkmarket.net** in the browser.

② Press Enter.

The website home page appears.

③ Click **Submit Your Site.**

The site submission page appears.

④ Type your e-mail address.

⑤ Type your password.

⑥ Type the website URL.

⑦ Click the **Category** pop-up menu and select the website category.

⑧ Click **Submit URL.**

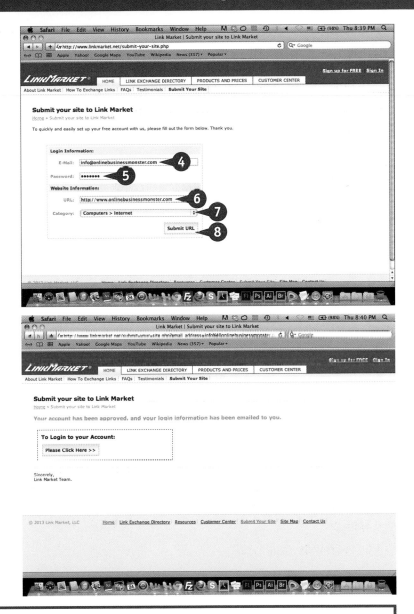

The account approval page appears.

Note: When Link Market sends you an e-mail to confirm your account, click the Confirmation link to activate it.

TIP

What is the difference between one-way and two-way links?

A *one-way* link points to someone else's page or website but there is no link back to your website. A *two-way* link refers to reciprocal links, where two websites exchange links so each site includes the partner's link. There are also *three-way* links, which refers to a group of websites linking to one other. For example, website 1 links to website 2, which links to website 3, which links to website 1, and so on. One-way link building is the best way to get rank because search engines such as Google consider one-way links quality links to your website. Two-way and three-way links are less important and should be used wisely to avoid any negative impact on the website.

Request a Link Exchange

You can search the Link Market directory for sites similar to yours and send link exchange requests. You add selected links to the Link Market cart and then use the cart to request link exchanges with the affiliated sites. Once the site owner approves the link exchange, the site owner adds the link to the website and you add this website's link to your website in return. You can manage your links and check their status under the My Account tab. Here you can also learn more about the Link Market platform by clicking the How to Exchange Links link.

Request a Link Exchange

1 Click **Link Exchange Directory.**

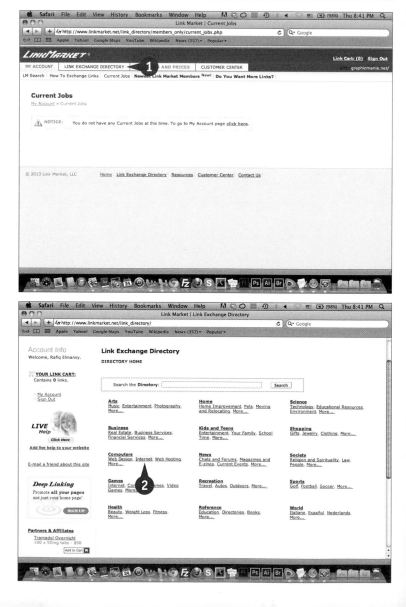

The link directory appears.

2 Select the category your website falls under.

The links in the directory appear.

3 Click **Add to Cart.**

4 Click **Link Cart.**

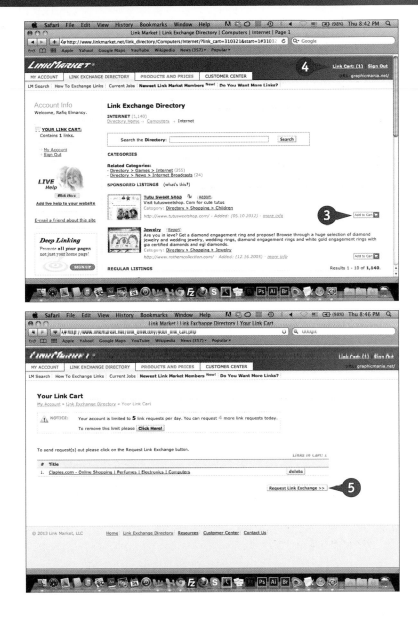

The Link Cart page appears.

5 Click **Request Link Exchange.**

How do I manage links in Link Market?

Under the Current Jobs tab, you can monitor link requests and the status of each one. There are three link status categories. Respond, which lets you know that a link request has been sent to you. Add Link, which notifies you that your partner has responded to your link request and has added your link to his or her site. And Remove Link, which means that the partner has not added your link or has removed it from his or her site.

CHAPTER 7

Working with Content

Your website's content is the most important part of your site and what your visitors seek when they come to your website via its URL, or via a search engine. Therefore, it is the first element that you need to optimize in your SEO process. Although you need to optimize the content so it's easily recognizable to search engine crawlers, it should also be unique and professional.

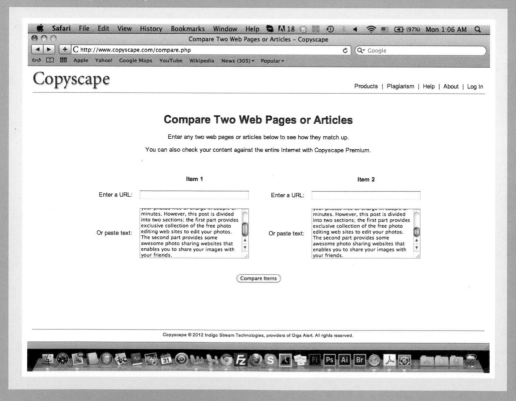

Build Optimized Content

Content is the main part of your website and it is the main factor that search engines use to rank and index your website. Even if you spend time and effort to optimize bad content, original, high-quality content will receive more traffic and be indexed by search engines much more easily. Having good content, however, does not mean that you need to forgo website optimization; the SEO process helps your content appear in the top of the search engine results page. Before you add your content, you should consider writing factors and how you will produce good content.

Provide Useful and Professional Content

When you write content for a website, you have to make sure that the content is unique and useful for your readers. Search engines reward high-quality content with higher ranking and better placement in search engine results. If your content is not good enough, it will eventually be buried in the search results page, as the search engine places better quality content above it.

Use Attractive and Representative Heading Titles

The first part of the content that your website visitor sees is the header. It is also the first part that the search engine checks when it begins to index your website. When you choose the content title, it should represent the topic discussed in the content. Additionally, the title should compel the user to click on your site and read through the content. A good title has to contain the most important keywords that you focus on in your article or post.

Write for Your Reader

Most website owners seeking better SEO positions make the terrible mistake of losing sight of their target, and, in turn, their readers' interest. When they lose their readers, they subsequently slip in the website rankings and lose website traffic. It is important to target your readers with topics that interest them and to use professional, high-quality

content. Your topics should include the keywords that you expect the user to use to find your content from search engines.

Drive Readers to Interact

When you build your website and add content, you have to consider the interaction with your readers, which is known as the *call-for-action* process. In this process, you try to add functions that help users interact with the website and the team behind it, such as providing a comments section, options for contacting you, and poll questions. You

can drive readers to interact with your website by asking them to share their experience with products and opinions about topics. This relationship builds a strong connection between your visitors and the website, helping you get more exposure in your website's market.

Use a Personal Voice When Possible

With some types of websites, such as blogs and personal sites, readers seek a personal experience with an expert and would like to hear the expert's opinions about specific topics. For example, you can visit an expert SEO blog to learn about his or her experience with special problems or tips to improve your website

Today was exciting...I finally had the time to scan in all the antique photos in my collection. From there, it was a matter of experimenting with making collages of them in my photo-editing program. I also scanned in theater tickets, programs, excerpts from old letters and diaries, and pressed flowers. Just a note; scanning pressed flowers leaves bits of crumbled flower on your scanner, but the end result is great.

indexing. A personal voice can help get the reader's attention because it represents friendly advice for someone in a similar position as the reader.

Check Duplicated Content

It is incredibly important to make sure your website content is not duplicated anywhere else on the web. Duplicated content can weaken your website and search engines may penalize it. Penalization can vary from reducing your website's rank to removing it from the search engine results page. Duplicated content happens when you copy others' content or other websites copy yours. While you do not have much control over the latter, the former is important because you do not want it to appear to search engines that your copied others' archived content. The process of copying content is called *plagiarism*.

Check Duplicated Content

1. Type **www.copyscape.com** in your web browser and press **Enter**.

The Copyscape website appears.

2. Type the URL that you would like to check for plagiarism.

3. Click **Go.**

The similar results appear.

4 Click one of the results.

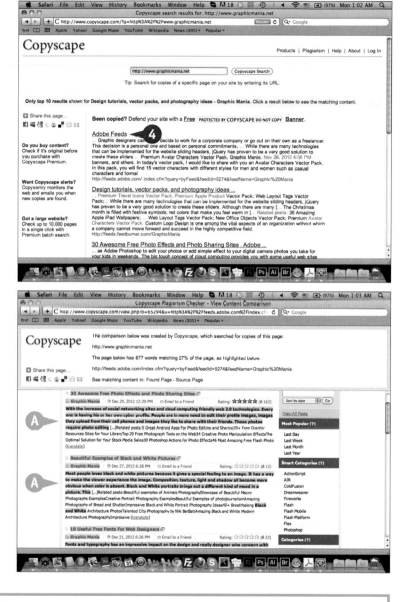

A The preview page appears
with the copied text
highlighted.

Are there any other plagiarism checkers?
Many free tools can help you to check website content for plagiarism and make sure that the content you add in your website is unique. You can use the Plagiarism Checker (www.dustball.com/cs/plagiarism.checker) to check copied versions of text, website content, and students' papers. Another option is Plagiarism Detect (http://plagiarism-detect.com/), a service that allows you to check the possible duplication of website links and text by uploading text files. Yet another is PlagTracker (www.plagtracker.com), which supports different languages and provides a comprehensive plagiarism checking process.

Compare Website Content

While duplicate content websites check specific links or content and compare them with the rest of the content on the Internet, Compare tools, such as Copyscape (www.copyscape.com/compare.php), help you identify similarities between two specific links or sections of text. You can use this tool if you know exact sections of website content that may have been copied from your site and you need to confirm it is identical without reading all the text on the website. This tool provides a match percentage for both sources and shows the similar keywords.

Compare Website Content

1 Type **www.copyscape.com/plagiarism.php** in your web browser and press Enter.

The plagiarism page appears.

2 Position your mouse pointer over **Products.**

3 Click **Free Content Comparison.**

The Compare page appears.

④ Type or paste the first section of text in the Item 1 field.

⑤ Type or paste the second section of text in the Item 2 field.

⑥ Click **Compare Items.**

Ⓐ The comparison results appear.

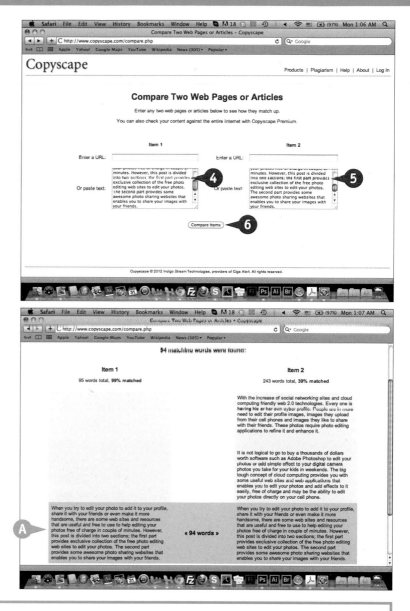

Are there any other compare tools?
You can use other tools to compare text, links, and HTML code to make sure that your website content is unique and it has not been copied from other places. DiffNow (www.diffnow.com) allows you to compare text and HTML code. Simply enter two website links, and DiffNow shows you the difference between the HTML code for both links. At www.comparemyfiles.com, you upload text files and compare them. In addition, you can find simpler tools at www.tareeinternet.com/scripts/comparison-tool, www.quickdiff.com, and www.diffchecker.com. Using compare tools is an important part of checking your website content's quality and originality before publishing it on your website.

Check Content Grammar and Spelling

If you are creating content for your website, you have to make sure that the content is free of grammar and spelling mistakes. These errors give your readers the impression that your website is not professional and they will leave it without the chance of returning again. From the search engine point of view, content with grammatical errors and typos may negatively impact your website ranking because your content does not appear to be high-quality content. Many online free tools, such as www.spellcheck.net, are available to help you check your website for typos and grammatical errors.

Check Content Grammar and Spelling

1 Type **www.spellcheck.net** in your web browser and press **Enter**.

The Spell Check form appears.

2 Type your text, or copy and paste it.

3 Click **Spell Check.**

The Spell Checker window appears with the spelling check results.

④ Click **Grammar.**

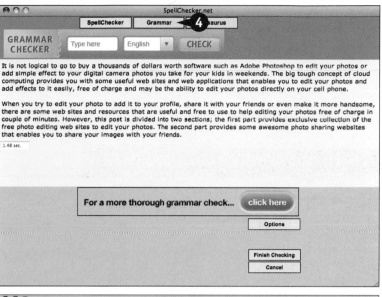

The grammar errors appear underlined.

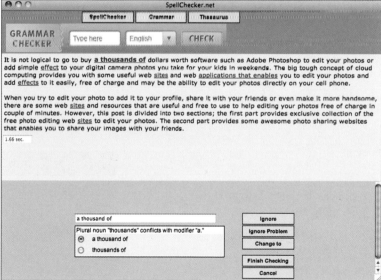

TIP

What other professional language editors can I use?

You can use a word processing application such as Microsoft Word or Apple Pages as a basic editor while you are writing your content. However, other applications, such as WhiteSmoke (www.whitesmoke.com), provide more comprehensive content editing tools. WhiteSmoke focuses on proofreading your content and provides statistics and evaluations for it. You can use it as a guide for proofreading your content, but it does not eliminate the need to do your own professional review.

Check Keyword Density

Search engine spiders index your content based on keywords that match the search query and website category. Given this, it is important to make sure the density of keywords in your website content meets the minimum, and does not exceed the maximum, amount required by the search engine. Tools to check different keywords in your content and its density are available. The Keyword Density Analysis Tool (www.internetmarketingninjas.com/seo-tools/keyword-density) is free; simply submit the content link and it searches different types of keywords.

Check Keyword Density

1 Type **www. internetmarketingninjas. com/seo-tools/keyword- density** in your web browser and press **Enter**.

The Keyword Density Analysis tool appears.

2 Type the website link.

3 Click **Ninja Check.**

The content keyword results appear.

④ Click **Show/Hide.**

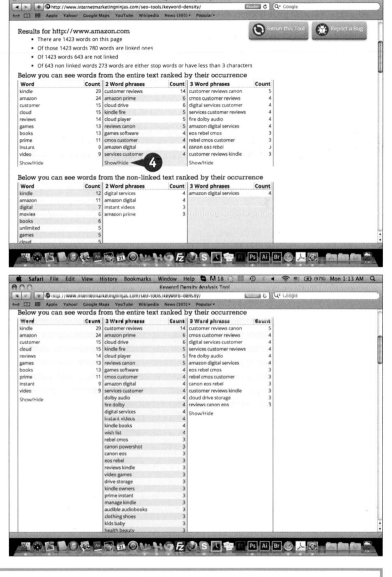

More keywords are revealed.

Are there other free keyword tools?

Yes, you can use other similar tools to check the keywords in your content, such as the SEO Book Keyword Density Analyzer tool at http://tools.seobook.com/general/keyword-density. With this tool, you can submit your website and get the number of repeating keywords and their density ratios within the entire content.

How do I add the keywords in the content naturally?

Make sure the keywords in your content flow naturally without affecting the quality of your content or annoying your website visitors while they are reading the article. Keeping your focus on high-quality content will help you achieve a high ranking in the search engine.

Create a RSS Feed with FeedBurner

The RSS (Really Simple Syndication) feed is a XML version of your website content and it is used by feed grabbers to get updates from your website. Creating the RSS feed is part of optimizing content because it makes it available to different web technologies, such as feed aggregators and news feeds. One of the comprehensive tools that allows you to create XML feed is Google's FeedBurner. It enables you to create feed for your website and generate a form your website users can use to join the feed and get updates about your new content directly via e-mail.

Create a RSS Feed with FeedBurner

1 Type **http://feedburner. google.com/** in your web browser and press **Enter**.

2 Type your e-mail address.

3 Type your password.

4 Click **Sign in.**

Note: You can create a new account if you do not already have one.

The FeedBurner home page appears.

5 Type the link for the website.

6 Click **Next.**

The next page appears.

7 Type the feed title.

8 Type the feed address.

9 Click **Next.**

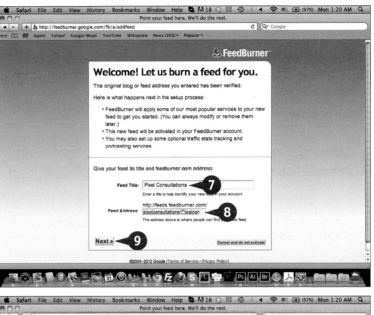

The Feed is created.

10 Click the **Skip directly to feed management** link to go to feed dashboard.

You can use the dashboard links to setup the feed and customize it.

TIP

How do I choose the best feed name and URL?

The feed name should represent your website and when users visit the feed directly from their web browsers or feed applications, they should see the name is the same as your website or reflects it. The feed URL is the link that users use to subscribe to your updates, either through their browsers or the feed applications that display site feeds directly on their computers or mobile devices. The URL should be easy to remember and reflect the website's content.

Create a Feed Subscription Form

In addition to using the feed link, users can subscribe to your feed through a subscription form on your website. The form lets users add their e-mails and get frequent updates about your website's new content directly in e-mails. A growing number of subscribers is a good indicator that your website is gaining readers who follow its updates frequently. You can invite website readers to subscribe to the website feed to get updates. This can help increase your number of subscribers.

Create a Feed Subscription Form

1. Type **http://feedburner.google.com/** in your web browser and press **Enter**.

2. Type your e-mail address.

3. Type your password.

4. Click **Sign in.**

The FeedBurner home page appears.

5. Click the feed title.

The Feed dashboard appears.

6 Click the **Publicize** tab.

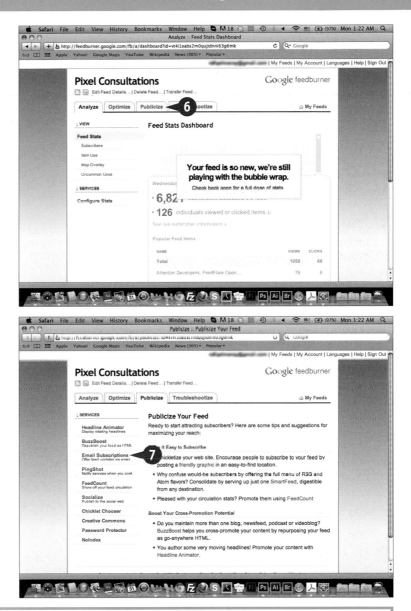

The Publicize tab home page appears.

7 Click **Email Subscriptions**.

TIPS

What are the RSS feed readers?
The RSS feed readers are tools that users can add to their favorite feed sites to grab website updates frequently. Some feed readers are online-based, such as www.google.com/reader, www.bloglines.com, and www.netvibes.com, which others are desktop-based such as Netnewswire www.netnewswireapp.com.

What is the PingShot service?
The PingShot service is an option in the FeedBurner dashboard that you can reach from the Publicize tab. After you activate this feature, PingShot starts to publish your website feed through other feed resources. You can use this feature to help spread the word about your feed updates to different feed readers.

continued ▶ 141

Y ou can customize the RSS feed subscription form by editing the code that FeedBurner provides. This customization can make the form compatible with your website design. Also, you can manage subscribers from Subscription Management, where you can view the subscribers' e-mail addresses and export them in an Excel Spreadsheet Comma Separate Value (CSV) format. You can customize the feed update e-mail through Email Branding, in the left menu. This option helps you customize the update e-mail title, logo image, and style format.

Create a Feed Subscription Form (continued)

The Email Subscriptions section appears.

8 Click **Activate**.

The Subscription Management page appears.

9 Scroll down the page.

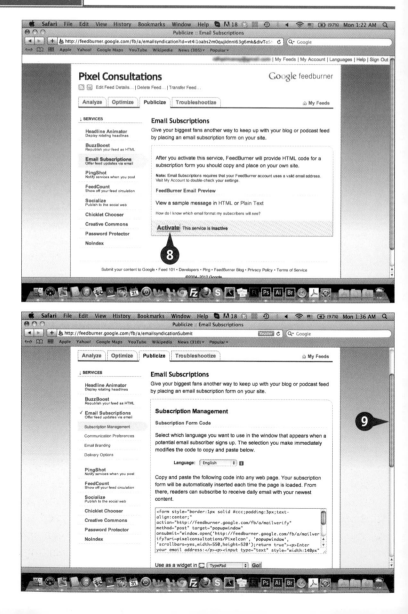

The Subscription Management settings appear.

⑩ Click the **Send me an email whenever people unsubscribe** option
(☐ changes to ☑).

⑪ Click **Save.**

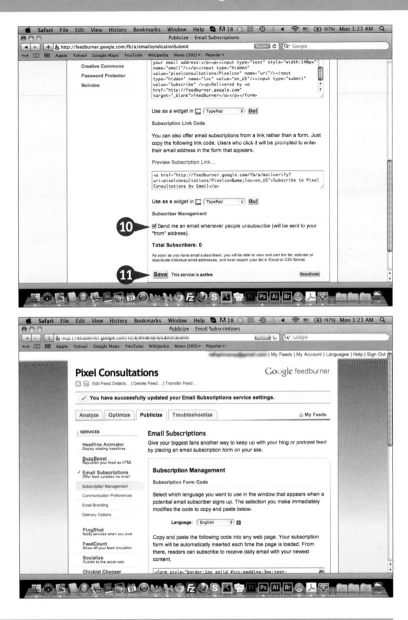

The feed customization settings are saved.

How do I promote the feed through Twitter?
You can tweet updates about your content to your social account on Twitter by selecting the Socialize option under the Publicize tab. When you activate this option, FeedBurner automatically publishes the feed updates to your Twitter account. You have an option to set up how the tweet message displays.

How do I show the feed count on my website?
Showing the feed count for your website often drives new visitors to join it. This feed count is a small count script that grabs the number of your feed subscribers from the FeedBurner account. You can activate the Feed Count and customize its settings under the Publicize tab.

Work with Professional Writing Services

Quality content is the most important part of your website. Not all website owners can write strong content for their sites. Given this, professional writing services that deliver website articles and content are available. With these websites, you submit a request for content about a specific topic and one of the website authors writes it for you based on your needs and requirements. Many of these sites provide templates that you can choose from, such as ones for product reviews, press releases, and lists. MediaPiston (www.mediapiston.com) is an example of one of these websites.

Work with Professional Writing Services

1 Type **www.mediapiston.com** in your browser and press **Enter**.

2 Click **Account Sign in**.

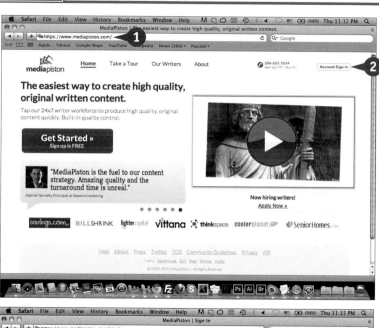

The Sign-in or create an account page appears.

3 Click **Odesk** to create an account using the www.odesk.com website.

Note: You need to create an account on www.odesk.com to hire a writer on MediaPiston.

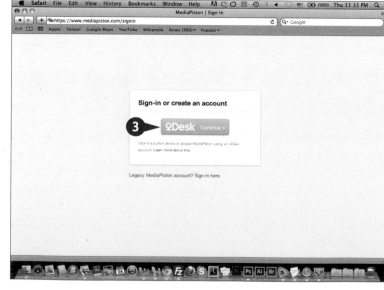

The MediaPiston home page appears.

④ Click **Create Order.**

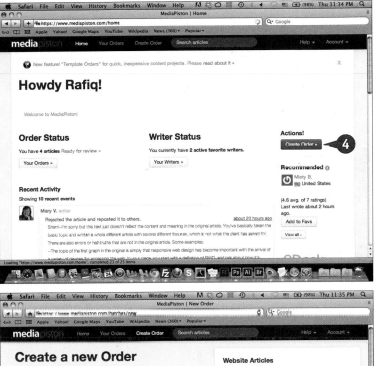

⑤ Fill in the Create a new Order form.

⑥ Click **Continue** to review your order and place it.

After your order is placed, one of the site authors will start writing the article for you.

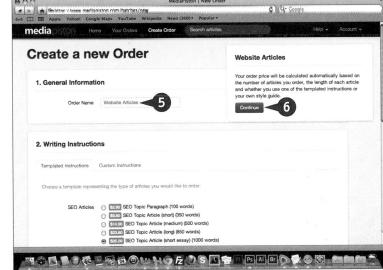

What are article templates?

You can choose among different templates with your article order. These templates include SEO articles, travel articles, and blog posts. You can also request marketing documents, such as product reviews, press releases, and social media posts.

How do I choose the article's length?

The length of the article should be suitable for your website audiences. For example, many blog posts stick to short articles or the audience loses interest in the topic. Alternatively, some websites require longer, more in-depth articles to earn high rankings in the search engines.

CHAPTER 8

Working with Google Analytics

Google Analytics is one of the most important tools in the search engine optimization (SEO) world; it helps you obtain information about website traffic, page views, where users click when they visit a website, and where visitors live. Google Analytics enables you to analyze a website to learn more about it. You can then apply this information to optimize your website.

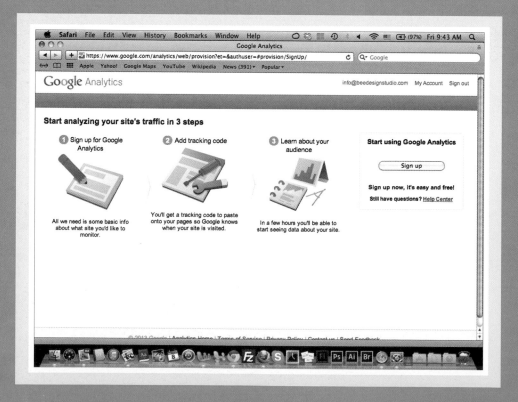

Create a Google Analytics Account

The Google account gives you access to different Google services, including Google Analytics. Each website or group of websites needs to have a *Google Analytics account*, which you create when you sign up. You can add one or more websites to track and analyze this account. You can also create a separate Analytics account for each website, which is known as a *Property*. For example, you can create a Google Analytics account for a specific website and its related sub-domains for better management. You can manage Analytics accounts and Properties from the *Admin* page.

Create a Google Analytics Account

1 Type **www.google.com/analytics** in your web browser and press **Enter**.

2 Click **Create an account.**

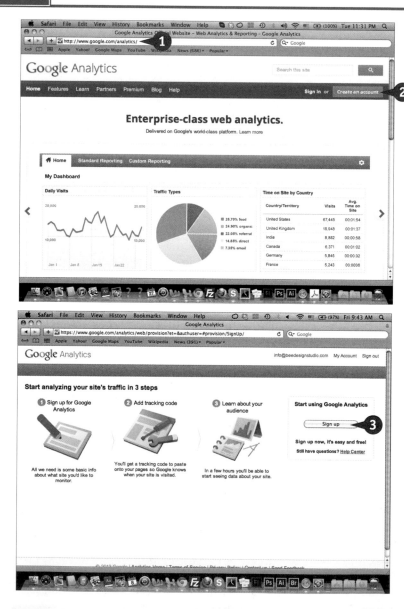

The Google Analytics sign up page appears.

3 Click **Sign up** to create a new Analytics account.

Note: If you are signing in with an existing account, you will be transferred to the Google Analytics home page.

The Account Administration page appears.

④ Click **Web Site.**

⑤ Type the website name to set up the name of the initial property in the account.

⑥ Type the website URL.

⑦ Click the **Industry Category** pop-up menu and select a website niche.

⑧ Click the **Reporting Time Zone** pop-up menus and select a country of origin and a time zone.

⑨ Scroll down the page.

The rest of the form fields appear.

⑩ Type the account name in the Account Name field.

⑪ Click the **Data Sharing Settings** option (☐ changes to ☑).

⑫ Click **Get Tracking ID.**

The Google Analytics Terms of Service page appears.

⑬ Click **I accept** to receive a Tracking ID.

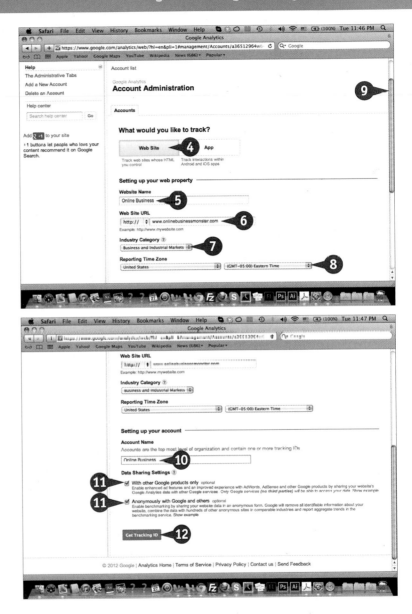

Where can I find the created accounts?
After you create the site accounts, the accounts appear on the Google Analytics home page. On this page, you can navigate through the site accounts and access any of the listed sites. You can also set specific site accounts as favorites so you can easily reach them later. You can show the account *Metrics* that display the statistics of each website. You can also search for sites and accounts using the Search field. This feature is very useful if you are reviewing multiple sites.

Install Google Analytics Code

*G*oogle Analytics tracking code is a snippet of code that Google assigns to each property or website to track its traffic and visitor information, such as the links visitors click, their web browser versions, their countries, and more. You can get the tracking code by clicking the Get Tracking ID button when you create a new account or property, or you can get it by accessing each account property's information page in *Analytics Admin*. Then, you can copy the code and paste it into your HTML page before the `</head>` closing tag.

Install Google Analytics Code

1 Click **Sign in** on Google Analytics.

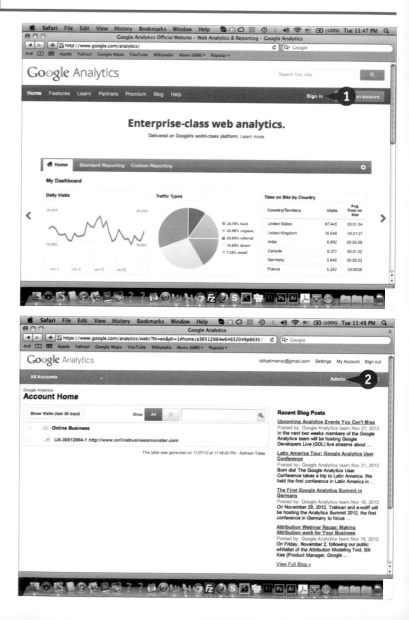

The Google Analytics Account Home page appears.

2 Click **Admin.**

The Account Administration
page appears.

3 Click the account; for
example, Online Business.

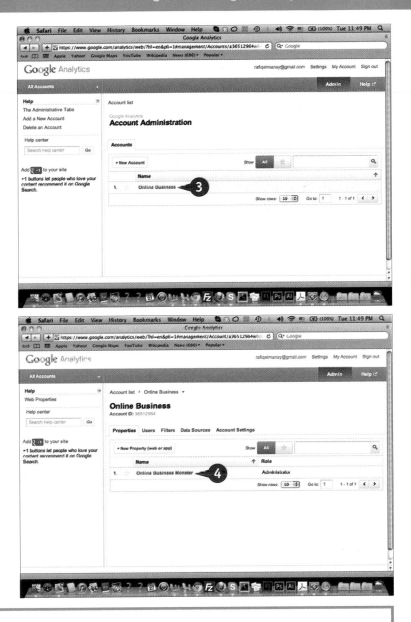

The All Accounts page
appears.

4 Click the property name; for
example, the Online Business
Monster property.

TIP

Where should I add the tracking code?
The Google Analytics tracking code is used to track the pages on which it is installed. For example, if you
install the code on index.html, the code will track the traffic and visitors on this specific page only. Thus,
you need to add the tracking code to each HTML page in your website. In some website structures, the
website header is added to a separate file that loads in index.html when you visit the website via your web
browser. In this case, you can add the code only in the header file and it will track the traffic from all the
website pages. Understanding the structure of your website helps you to avoid multiple insertions or
duplicate code on the website.

continued ▶ 151

The Google Analytics code provides a trusted way to track your website traffic and visitor information. This information is essential for the SEO process because it allows you to monitor website traffic, the high SERP (search engine results page) content, and other information. You can use this information to refine the SEO process for your website and track the progress of each optimization task to determine the best SEO techniques for your website. For example, you can use the Analytics data to figure out the SERP keywords that bring the most traffic to your website and other keywords that you can optimize to get better SERP rankings.

Install Google Analytics Code (continued)

The Accounts Properties page appears

5 Click the **Tracking Info** tab.

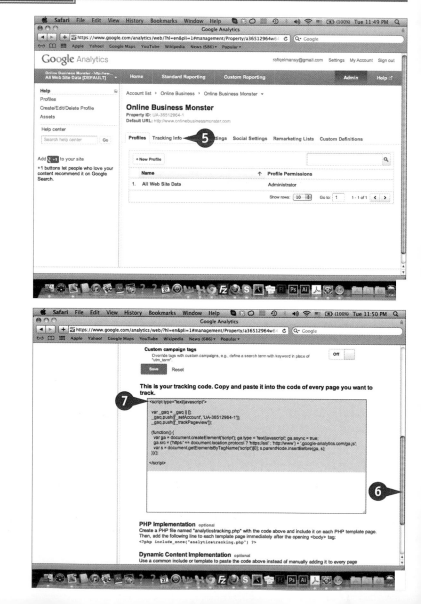

The Tracking tab is active.

6 Scroll down to the tracking code section.

7 Click and drag to select and then press ⌘+C (Ctrl+C) to copy the tracking code.

8 In the HTML document, position the mouse pointer before the `</head>` closing tag.

9 Press Enter.

```
<! DOCTYPE html>
<html>
<head>
<title>My Website Title</title>
<meta name="description" content="Page Description">
<meta name="keywords" content="Keyword1, Keyword2, Keyword3">
<meta name="author" content="Website author name">
<meta name="copyright" content="2012">

</head>
<body>
<p><img src="/image_name.jpg" title="image title" alt="image description"  />
<br/>
image information</p>
Hello World!content="2012">
</body>
</html>
```

10 Press ⌘+V (Ctrl+V) to paste the tracking code.

11 Press ⌘+S (Ctrl+S) to save the document.

After the code is inserted, it takes around few days to display the website statistics.

```
<! DOCTYPE html>
<html>
<head>
<title>My Website Title</title>
<meta name="description" content="Page Description">
<meta name="keywords" content="Keyword1, Keyword2, Keyword3">
<meta name="author" content="Website author name">
<meta name="copyright" content="2012">
<script type="text/javascript">

  var _gaq = _gaq || [];
  _gaq.push(['_setAccount', 'UA-36512964-1']);
  _gaq.push(['_trackPageview']);

  (function() {
    var ga = document.createElement('script'); ga.type = 'text/javascript'; ga.async = true;
    ga.src = ('https:' == document.location.protocol ? 'https://ssl' : 'http://www') +
'.google-analytics.com/ga.js';
    var s = document.getElementsByTagName('script')[0]; s.parentNode.insertBefore(ga, s);
  })();

</script>
</head>
<body>
<p><img src="/image_name.jpg" title="image title" alt="image description"  />
<br/>
image information</p>
```

TIPS

Why do the code results not appear right away?
When you first install the Analytics code, it takes a couple of days before you will receive a complete report for the website data. When the word "Verified" appears next to the website in the Analytics accounts page, it means the code has been installed correctly.

How do I install the code in PHP sites?
For websites that use PHP as a coding language, Analytics code is installed in a different way. In this case, you want to create a file on the server with the name analyticstracking.php. This file should include the Analytics tracking code, which you place after the opening of the `<body>` tag using the code `<?php include_ once("analyticstracking.php") ?>`.

Create a New Analytics Account

Google Analytics allows you to create multiple accounts on your dashboard and each account can include one or more properties. You can use this option to organize your Analytics dashboard, especially when you have large list of websites to track. For example, you can create an account for a specific website and its *sub-domains*. The sub-domains are websites hosted under the main website server and domain name. For example, you can have the website www.sitename.com with the sub-domains http://faq.sitename.com and http://help.sitename.com. Arranging the websites help you to get better tracking for the sites and share it with your teamwork.

Create a New Analytics Account

① Click **Admin** on the Google Analytics home page.

The Accounts Administration page appears.

② Click **New Account.**

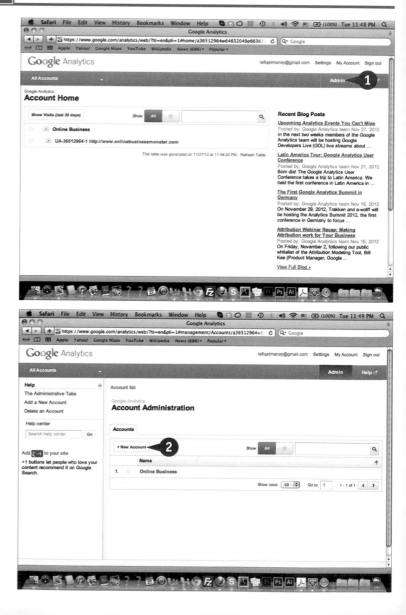

The New Account page
appears.

3 Click **Web Site.**

4 Type the website name to set
up the name of the initial
property in the account.

5 Type the website URL.

6 Click the **Industry Category**
pop-up menu and select a
website niche; for example,
Healthcare.

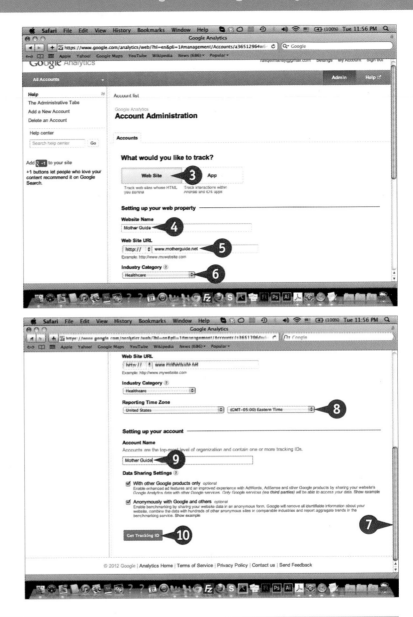

7 Scroll down the page.

8 Click the **Reporting Time Zone**
pop-up menus and select a country
or origin and a time zone.

9 Type the account name in the
Account Name field.

10 Click **Get Tracking ID.**

The Google Analytics Terms of
Service page appears.

11 Click **I accept** to receive a
Tracking ID.

TIP

How many site accounts can I create in Google Analytics?
Google Analytics allows you to use up to 50 site accounts to manage your websites. In each account, you
can add multiple properties. In some cases, you may need to create a separate Google Analytics account for
a specific website. For example, if you sell the website, the buyer will lose all the old analytics details when
he adds the website to his own Google Analytics account. Therefore, in order for the buyer to preserve the
old analytics, you should give the buyer your whole Google Analytics account. In this case, it is advisable
to have a separate Google Analytics account for this specific website.

Add a New Property Website

Under each site account in Google Analytics, you can add one or more websites, which are known as *Properties*. These Properties appear under the main site account in the Admin page. Each website has its own tracking code, which you will need to install in the website in order to track the website statistics and analyze them in Google Analytics. You can use this Accounts and Properties structure to organize your sites and their related domains and sub-domains. Also, you can use it to organize related websites under the main site account.

Add a New Property Website

1 Click **Admin** on the Google Analytics home page.

The Account Administration page appears.

2 Click an account; for example, Online Business.

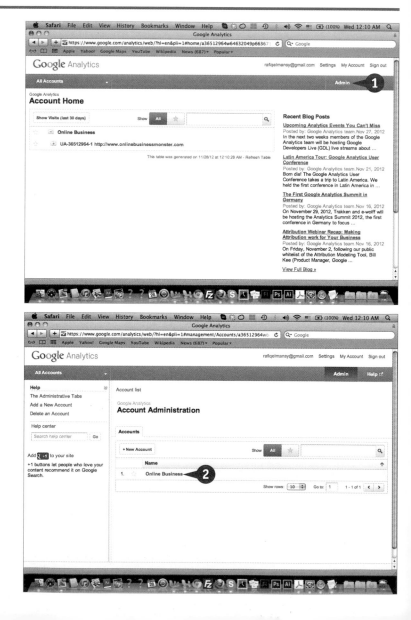

The Account page appears.

3 Click **+ New Property (web or app)**.

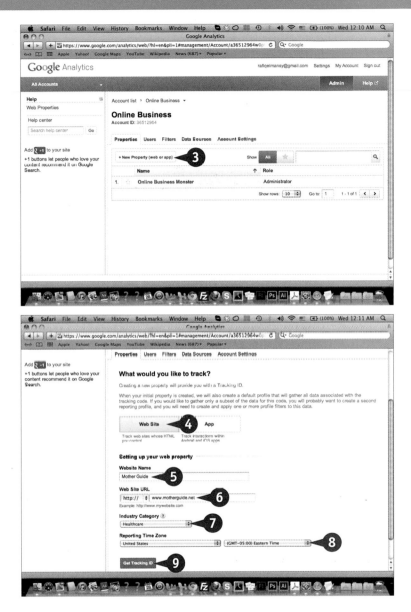

The new property page appears.

4 Click **Web Site**.

5 Type the website name to set up the name of the initial property in the account.

6 Type the website URL.

7 Click the **Industry Category** pop-up menu and select a website niche.

8 Click the **Reporting Time Zone** pop-up menus and select a country or origin and a time zone.

9 Click **Get Tracking ID.**

After receiving the tracking code, you can install it on your website.

Can I track mobile application statistics?
Yes, you can create a tracking code for mobile application by clicking **App** from the new properties page. You can use the tracking code to get statistic information about your Android or iOS application and display it in your Google Analytics account. You can use this code with multiple versions of the application, and you can also install it to multiple applications.

View Website Analytics

Standard Reporting appears on the Analytics page. It includes information on *Unique Visitors,* counted once during their visits, and *New Visitors,* visiting for the first time.

Page views indicates how many pages visitors view. *Page/Visit* shows the number of pages each user visits. *Avg. Visit Duration* shows how long users browse the website, and *Bounce Rate* indicates the percentage of users visiting the page and then leaving without viewing other pages.

View Website Analytics

1 Click **All Web Site Data** or your own profile name from the Analytics Account Home page.

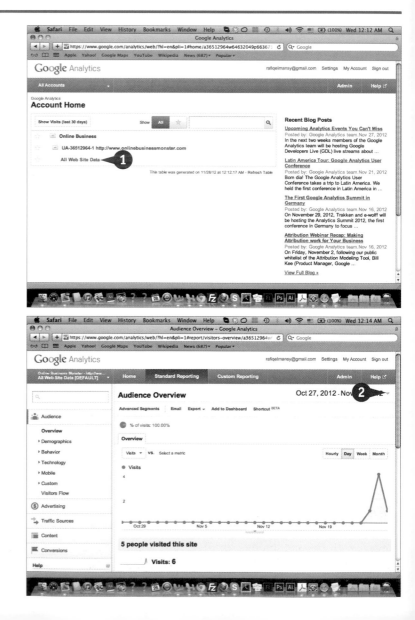

The Standard Reporting page appears.

2 Click the **Data Range** down arrow (▾).

The Data Range timeline appears.

③ Click a starting date to set the start of the data range.

④ Click an ending date to set the end date for data range.

⑤ Click **Apply.**

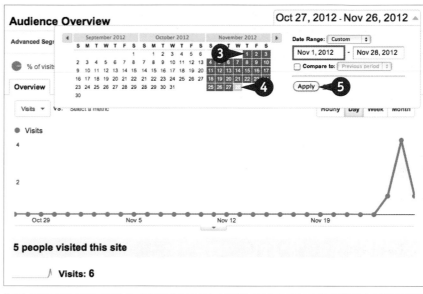

The website statistics for the period chosen appear.

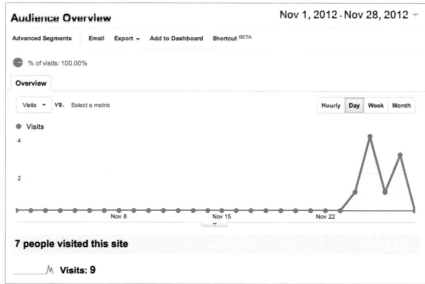

What is the different between Standard and Custom Reporting?
The Standard Reporting tab displays the default information for visits, unique visitors, and page views. This view appears when you access the website analytics. The Custom Reporting tab enables you to create a new customized report with specific information. You can create multiple custom reports for different purposes and web analytics.

How can I share Google Analytics reports?
Google Analytics lets you share reports by e-mail or download them in various formats. You can click **Export** to save the report on your computer in CSV, TSV, TSV for Excel, and PDF formats. From the Standard Reports tab, you can click **Email** from the menu bar to send a report to e-mail recipients.

Add Multiple Users

Google Analytics allows you to add multiple users to specific accounts and allow them to view Account Properties statistics. Newly created users can be the *User* or *Administrator*. You can set the specific website *Profile* to display for the User. The Profile shows property data in a custom way; for example, it can show only the traffic from Google organic search. The Administrator account can view all the available properties for the account. The multiple users feature is very useful when you are part of a team that would like to share website statistics.

Add Multiple Users

1 Click an account on the Account Administration page.

The Account page appears.

2 Click the **Users** tab.

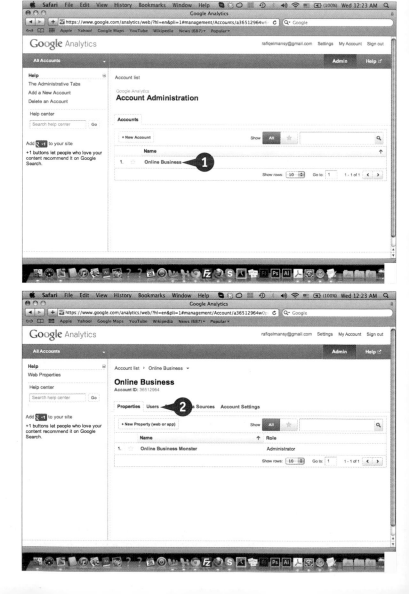

Working with Google Analytics

The Users page appears.

3 Click the **+ New User** tab.

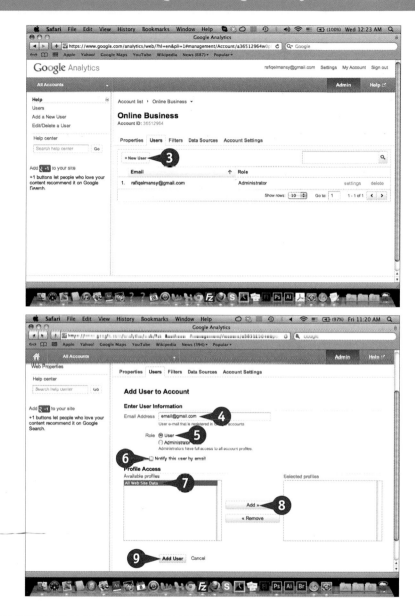

The new user form appears.

4 Type the user's e-mail address.

5 Click the **User** role option
(○ changes to ◉).

6 Click the **Notify this user by email**
check box (☐ changes to ☑).

7 Click your profile name.

8 Click **Add.**

9 Click **Add User.**

The user will receive a notification
and then be able to see the website
reports.

Under what conditions do I choose the User or the Administrator role?

The User role has very limited capabilities in comparison with the Administrator role. The User role cannot edit the Analytics settings or add new users. The Administrator role has similar privileges as the owner. The Administrator can access all reports, modify settings, and add new users.

How can I create or edit a website profile?

On the Accounts page, click an account. Select the current profile to edit, or click **+New Profile** to create a new profile that will take you to the profile set up. In the new profile, you can add users, filters, custom alerts, scheduled e-mails, shortcuts, and set Goals.

View Real-Time Statistics

*R*eal-time statistics show you live updates for website analytics. When you click the Property analytics, you get gathered information and statistics about the website. By clicking the Real-Time option on the Analytics web page, you can view live information about the website's current number of visitors, the locations of those visitors, the traffic sources these visitors come use, and the currently visited content. You can also click the Overview link to view a summary of all live data.

View Real-Time Statistics

1 Click **All Web Site Data** or your own profile name on the Google Analytics Account Home page.

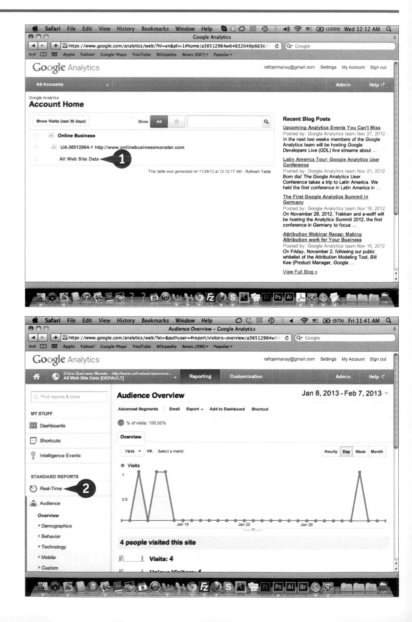

The Website Analytics page appears.

2 Click **Real-Time** under Standard Reports.

The Real-Time submenu expands.

3 Click **Overview.**

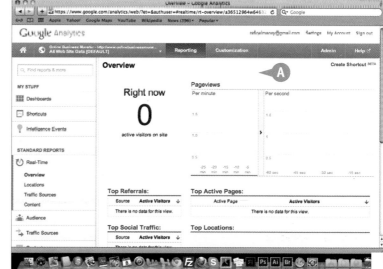

A The Real-Time Overview statistics expand, showing live information about the website visitors.

Why are the Real-Time statistics important?

In the SEO process, you want live analytics about the website. For example, you may need to know the time when the website receives the most traffic to determine the best time to publish website content. The live statistics also give you an idea of the type of content that visitors visit through the day.

What information can I obtain from the Real-Time statistics?

From the Real-Time overview, you can check the current traffic for the website and number of page views. You can check the origin of the website traffic and location of visitors. You can also learn about the search keywords that display the website on search engine results pages.

Exclude Traffic from a Specific IP

Every Google Analytics profile allows you to add *Filters*, which allow you to exclude specific data from appearing in the profile. For example, you can use them to hide traffic information from your *IP*. The Internet Protocol (IP) address is a set of numbers assigned to each website. Usually, you need to check the website frequently while testing and developing content from your own browser setting. The analytics information about your own website visits is not important and may be misleading. Using Filters to exclude your IP data can help you to get more accurate traffic data.

Exclude Traffic from a Specific IP

1 Click the account name in the Account Admin page.

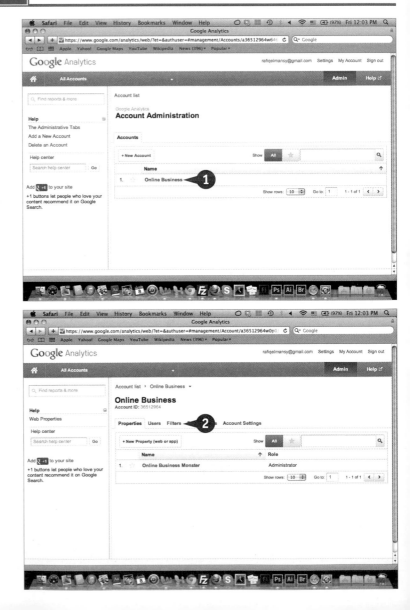

The account admin page appears.

2 Click **Filters.**

The Filters page appears.

③ Click **+New Filter**.

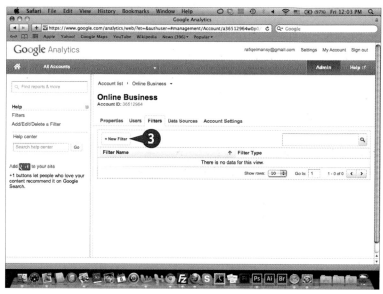

The New Filter page appears.

④ Type your filter name.

⑤ Click the **Predefined filter** option
(○ changes to ◉).

⑥ Click the **Filter type** pop-up menu
and select Exclude.

⑦ Click the pop-up menu and select
traffic from the IP addresses.

⑧ Click the pop-up menu and select
that are equal to.

⑨ Type the IP address in the fields.

⑩ Click **All Web Site Data**.

⑪ Click **Add**.

⑫ Click **Save**.

The filter is added and will apply to
all the web site data.

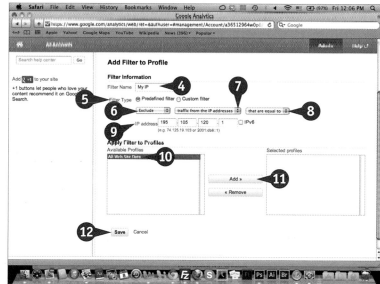

TIPS

What type of filter can I create?
The Filters options allow you to create filters based on
different criteria. Each criterion can exclude or include
traffic from specific sources. For example, you can
choose to exclude traffic from a specific ISP domain,
IP address, subdirectory of a specific website, and
hostname. You can also apply multiple filters to the
same profile and apply different criteria for each filter.

**Can I apply the same filter for more than
one profile?**
Yes, you can create a filter and apply it to
multiple profiles in the same account. You can do
this by clicking the **Filters** tab in the Analytics
account. This option is helpful for creating global
filters that you can use with different profiles.

Set a Conversion Goal

Google Analytics' Conversion Goals enable you to measure if you are achieving your objectives. It tracks actions giving you ideas about your progress in achieving a specific result. This goal can be the time users spend on your website or the number of page views. You set goals at the profile level and are limited to four sets of goals. Each set is limited to five goals, which means that each profile has a maximum of 20 goals. The four types of goals are *URL Destination*, *Visit Duration*, *Page/View*, and *Event*.

Set a Conversion Goal

1 Click **Goals** or your own profile name on the All Web Site Data page.

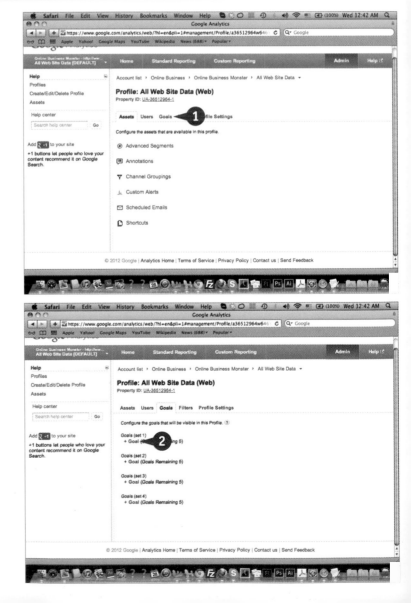

The Goals section appears.

2 Click **+Goal** under the Goals (set 1).

The Goal setting appears.

3 Type your goal in the Goal Name field.

4 Click the **Visit Duration** option under the Goal Type section (○ changes to ⦿).

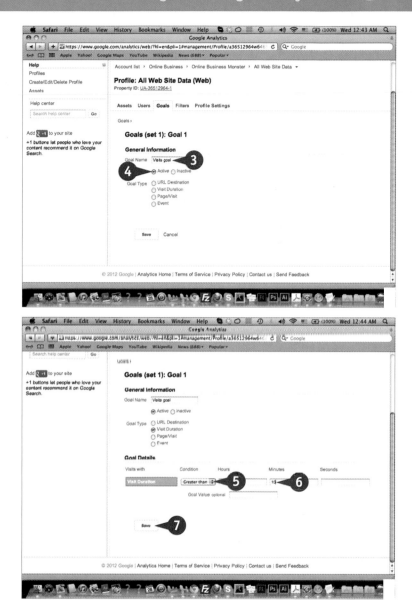

The Visit Duration setting appears.

5 Click the **Condition** pop-up menu and select Greater than.

6 Type the hours and/or minutes in the Hours and Minutes fields; for example, type 10 in the Minutes field.

7 Click **Save**.

The goal appears in the Goals tab as one of the goals of your account and also on the Analytics home page under the Conversions section.

TIP

What is a URL Destination goal?
The URL Destination goal tracks the traffic for a specific URL. You can choose from three match types. The *Head Match* is a good choice for shopping pages that have parameters in the end of the URL. *Exact Match* matches the exact characters in the URL and it is suitable for static URLs. The *Regular Expression Match* uses special characters for more flexibility. You can choose one of these options based on the URL you use.

Find Website Keywords

One of the advantages of using Google Analytics is it allows you to find the keywords that give you the best ranking in different search engines. Once you identify these keywords, you can build new content that targets them to increase search engine traffic. You can also monitor new keywords to see if they increase traffic to your website. This feature is very helpful and an essential part of the SEO process, because it shows you the direct impact of keyword optimization on the website traffic.

Find Website Keywords

1 Click **All Web Site Data,** or your own profile name on the Analytics Account Home page.

The Standard Reporting page appears.

2 Click **Traffic Sources** to expand the menu.

3 Click **Sources.**

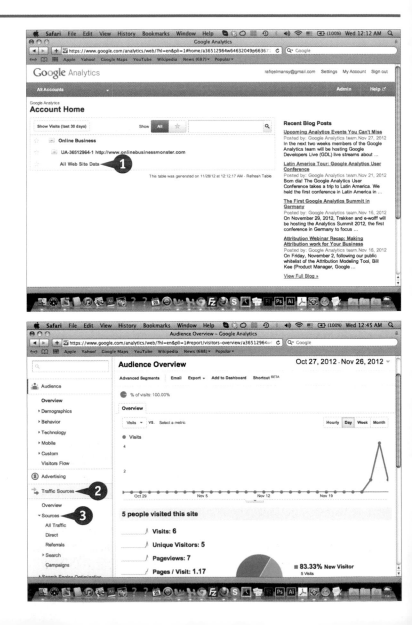

The Sources link expands.

④ Click **Search.**

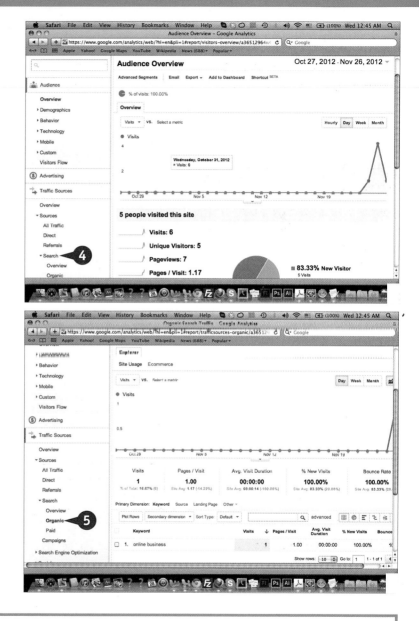

The Search link expands.

⑤ Click **Organic.**

The organic traffic appears in the statistics.

What is the Search Engine Optimization link?

In addition to the Traffic Sources data, you can maximize your knowledge of website keywords and traffic using the Search Engine Optimization link. This link allows you to link between Google Analytics and Google Webmaster Tools, which gives you more information about the website links and keyword queries. These queries are what users use to search for website pages. When you link Google Analytics with Webmasters Tools, you can check the queries in more depth. Also, you will be able to learn about website home page and where users go when they visit your website.

CHAPTER 9

Using Search Engine Webmaster Tools

Google Webmaster Tools is one of the resources search engine optimization (SEO) experts use to track website performance, sitemap status, crawling errors, and links.

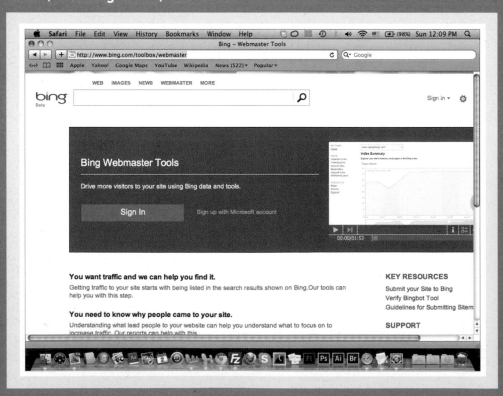

Add a Website to a Google Webmaster Account

As with Google Analytics, you need to have a Google account to use Google Webmaster Tools. When you access Webmaster Tools, you can add one or more websites to your account, each with a separate dashboard and analytics. To add a website, you need to use the Add a Site link and then verify the website to identify that you are the owner. After you add your website to Webmaster Tools, it takes a few days for your site's statistics to appear in your website account.

Add a Website to a Google Webmaster Account

1 Type **www.google.com/ webmasters/tools/** in your web browser and press **Enter**.

The Google Webmaster Tools sign in page appears.

2 Type your e-mail address.

3 Type your password.

4 Click **Sign In**.

Note: If you do not have a Google account, you can create one by clicking **Sign Up.**

The Google Webmaster home page appears.

5 Click **Add a Site.**

The Add a site dialog box appears.

6 Type your website URL; for example, www.buzz3d.net.

7 Click **Continue** to move forward with verifying your website.

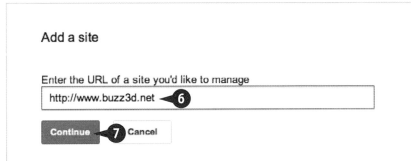

TIP

What is the different between Google Analytics and Google Webmaster Tools?
The initial different between Google Analytics and Google Webmaster Tools is Google Analytics focuses on showing website analytics related to traffic, the number of visitors, and the number of page views. Google Webmaster Tools is a group of tools you can use to analyze the website from a crawling point of view. That is, you can check for crawling errors, and how the Google bots interact with the website and show its content. You can also use Google Webmaster tools to set up how frequently your website will be crawled and to learn about different link types inside your site.

Verify Your Website for Google Webmaster Tools

One important process when adding your website to Webmaster Tools is verifying that you are the website owner. You can do this by downloading the verification HTML document and uploading it to the root path of your website on the server. First upload the file using an FTP application such as FireFTP or FileZilla. After uploading the document, return to the website verification page on Webmaster Tools and click Verify to verify your website. You will now be able to see statistics for the website and its crawling status on the website dashboard on Google Webmaster.

Verify Your Website for Google Webmaster Tools

1 Click **Manage site** next to aboutwordpress.net.

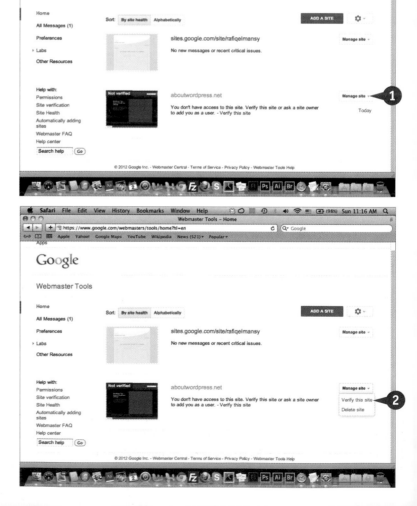

The Manage site pop-up menu appears.

2 Click **Verify this site.**

The Verify your ownership page appears.

③ Click the **this HTML verification file** link to download the file on your computer.

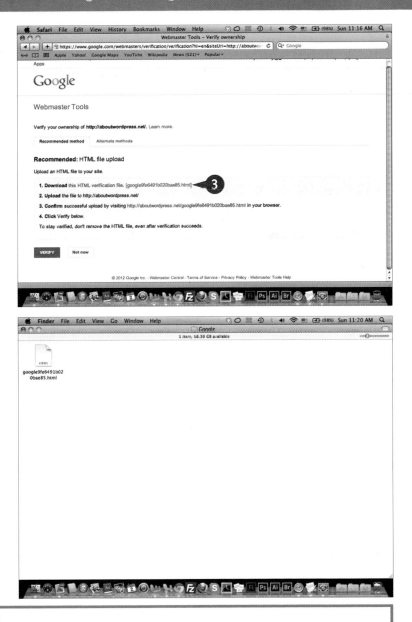

The document is saved on your computer. You can upload the document to your website server root folder by using any FTP application.

What are the site verification options?
The default verification of ownership option is to download the verification HTML document and upload it to your website server on the root path. You can access it here by typing **www.*name.com*/Google_ vertification_file.html**. There are also three other methods. The first is using HTML tag: you need to add code to the website home page HTML. The second is using your Google Analytics account, and the third is providing Domain Name Provider information. In this method, you need to sign in using the domain registrar information. You can choose either the default method or one of the three alternatives to verify your website based on your knowledge and experience.

continued ▶ 175

A fter you verify your website for Google Webmaster tools, you can view the website statistics on the dashboard that the Webmaster tools create for your website. You will need to wait for few days to allow Google Webmaster to collect the available information about your website and display it in the website dashboard. Unlike the Google Analytics tool that display updates about the website statistics on daily basis, the Google Webmaster tools website information takes around two to three days to appear on the dashboard.

Verify Your Website for Google Webmaster Tools (continued)

④ Upload the document to your website's root folder.

You can click the Browser icon to go back to the verification page in Step **3**.

⑤ Click **Verify.**

The successful verification page appears.

6 Click **Continue.**

The website dashboard appears.

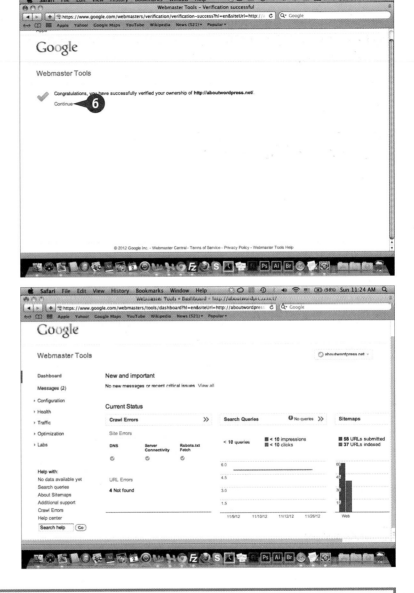

TIPS

How do I delete a website from Google Webmaster Tools?
You can easily delete a website from the Google Webmaster Tools home page. All you need to do is click the **Manage Site** pop-up menu, click **Delete Site**, and then confirm your choice to remove the website.

What are the Compact and Comfortable views?
The Compact and Comfortable views are the two main types of website views on the Google Webmaster Tools home page. The Compact mode displays only the name of the website, and the Comfortable mode displays a preview of the website. In the Comfortable mode, a small Verified notice on the website thumbnail verifies the website's status when verified.

Submit a Sitemap to Google Webmaster Tools

Google Webmaster Tools allows you to submit one or more XML sitemaps. Theses sitemaps help the search engines crawl your website more efficiently to index its links. It also helps search engines update their information about your website's keywords, images, categories, and more. To submit a website sitemap, upload it in XML to your website server. Next, add the sitemap path in Google Webmaster Tools. Then, submit the sitemap path through the Sitemap link in the left menu.

Submit a Sitemap to Google Webmaster Tools

1 Click **Optimization** under the Dashboard section.

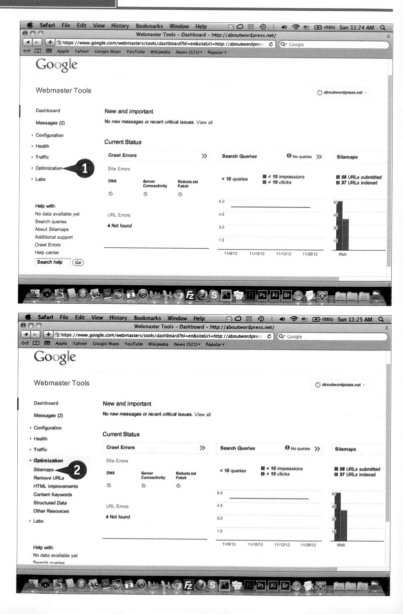

The Optimization menu expands.

2 Click **Sitemaps.**

The Sitemaps page appears.

3 Click **Add/Test Sitemap.**

The Sitemaps submission form appears.

4 Type the path of the sitemap.

5 Click **Submit Sitemap.**

A couple days after the sitemap is submitted, you will see its links indexed in the website dashboard. You can reach the sitemaps from the Sitemap link in the Optimization left menu.

TIPS

What is the Test Sitemap?

The Test Sitemap feature enables you to test a website by viewing the links indexed in the sitemap along with any errors. After you make sure the sitemap is acceptable, you can finish your test and then submit it for crawlers to index. With this feature, you do not have to wait until the sitemap is crawled to check for errors.

How much time does it take to index sitemap links?

It takes a few days to index its links. Typically, not all links are indexed due to crawler factors. Therefore, it is normal to find the number of indexed links less than the original sitemap links. The large difference can indicate a problem in the sitemap.

Configure Google Webmaster Tools Settings

You use Google Webmaster Tools Settings to configure crawling options for your website. You can target users in a specific country. You can also choose whether you want to include www. For example, you can set the domain name to http://website.com instead of www.website.com. Last, you can choose the crawling rate, which determines how frequently your website is crawled. You can let Google determine the crawling rate or you can set it manually.

Configure Google Webmaster Tools Settings

1 Click **Configuration** under the Dashboard section.

The Configuration menu expands.

2 Click **Settings.**

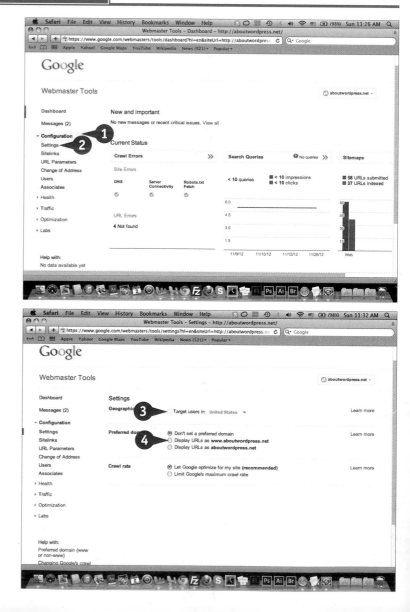

The Settings page appears.

3 Click to deselect the **Target users in** option (☑ changes to ☐).

4 Click the **Display URLs as www.aboutwordpress.net** option (○ changes to ◉).

The Save button appears

5 Click **Save.**

6 Click the **Limit Google's maximum crawl rate** option (○ changes to ◉).

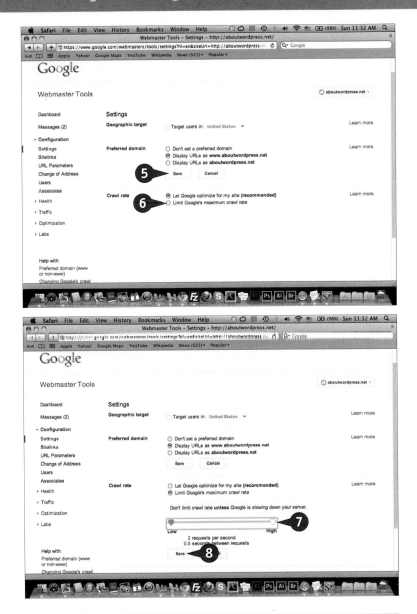

The crawl rate slider appears.

7 Click and drag the slider to **High.**

8 Click **Save.**

Your new settings are saved and applied to the website.

TIPS

Why should I choose a geographical target?
If your website is receiving traffic from a specific country, you want to set a geographical target for this country. The search engine will display your website more efficiently in the search results page for visitors from these countries.

What is the best crawling rate for my website?
A high crawling rate ensures fast crawling for your website updates, but it creates load on the server, slowing it down. Therefore, a high crawling rate is not recommended if you are running your website on a slow server. If you are not sure if your web server can handle this new rate, select the Let Google optimize for my site default option.

Check for Google Crawling Errors

One of Google Webmaster Tools' most important features is helping you find out and trace crawling errors. When search engine spiders crawl your website to index it, they may find errors or problems that prevent them from indexing it properly. These errors can be missing pages or pages crawlers cannot access. Also, Google Webmaster Tools can show you if there are any errors related to the server. Click Health under the Dashboard section to access the Crawl Errors page. Address the errors and then return to the Crawl Errors page and mark them as fixed.

Check for Google Crawling Errors

1 Click **Health** under the Dashboard section.

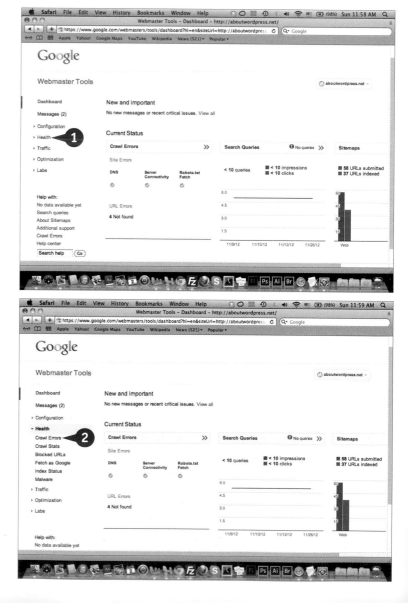

The Health menu expands.

2 Click **Crawl Errors.**

The Site Errors page appears.

3 Scroll down to the URL Errors section.

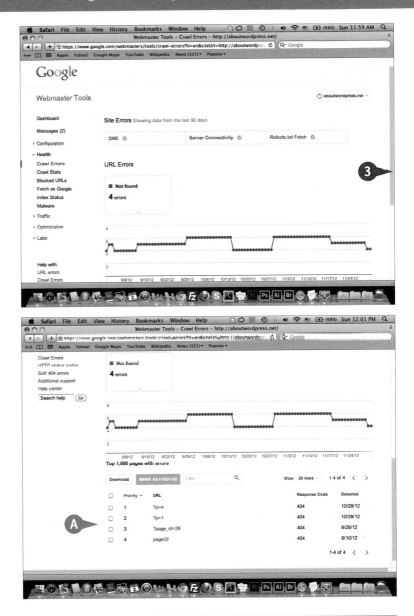

A The list of pages the crawler could not find appears.

What is the 404 error?

The 404 (Not Found) error is a normal when you have a lot of traffic on your server. These errors are client-side errors. For example, they can occur when a browser cannot access a specific page, or if a user enters the wrong page URL, the 404 (Not Found) error appears.

What is the Crawler Stats page?

The Crawler Stats page shows you statistics for the search engine crawler, such as the number of pages crawled per day, the crawled content downloaded in kilobytes, and the time the crawler spends downloading a page in milliseconds. The faster the search bots crawl your website, the more content will be crawled and indexed in a shorter time.

Preview Your Website as Googlebots

M any factors affect how a search engine sees your website. Sometimes, the website looks correct to you but not in the search engine. The Google Webmaster Tools Fetch feature shows you your website the way Google sees it. You can fetch the website home page or any internal pages. To do this, open the Fetch page and add the path of the page that you would like to fetch, or just leave the fetch field blank to preview your website's home page. After previewing the page, submit it to Google to index if it has not been indexed.

Preview Your Website as Googlebots

1 Click **Health** under the Dashboard section.

The Health menu expands.

2 Click **Fetch as Google.**

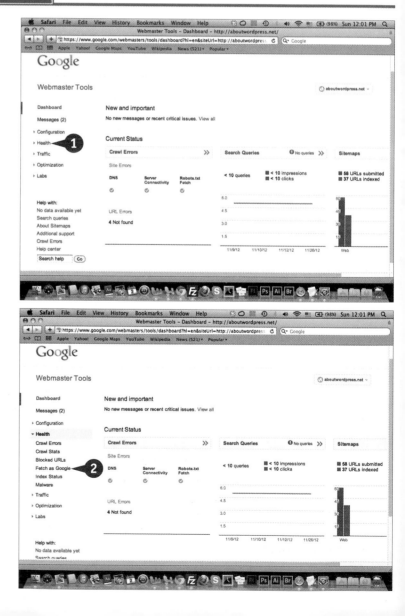

The Fetch as Google page appears.

3 Type your web page path; for example, best-free-google-adsense-plugins-for-wordpress.

4 Click **Fetch**.

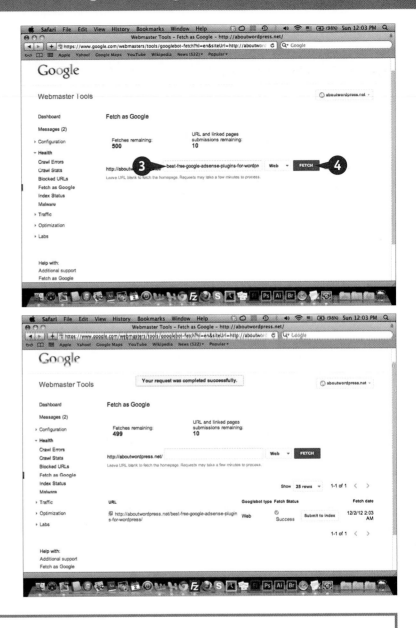

The Fetch results appear.

TIP

What are Sitelinks?
When the search engine displays your website in the search results page, it often displays the internal links from your website it deems useful to the user. These links are known as *Sitelinks*. You can view them from the Sitelinks link under the Configure menu in the website dashboard. While Google automatically chooses these links, you can choose to remove, or demote, specific links. For example, you may choose to remove the About us or Contact us page from displaying in the Sitelinks section and include only those links for useful content pages.

Submit a Website to the Bing Webmaster

Similar to Google Webmaster Tools, Bing Webmaster lets you add your website, submit sitemaps, and track website crawling data indexed by Bing crawlers. When you submit your website to Bing, it is crawled by both Bing and Yahoo crawlers because both search engines are linked together. It is important to consider your website indexing status on Bing's search engine because it reflects traffic to your website from Bing and Yahoo search engine users. You can sign in to Bing Webmaster using your Microsoft username and password or you can create an account if you do not already have one.

Submit a Website to the Bing Webmaster

1 Type **www.bing.com/toolbox/ webmaster** in your web browser and press Enter.

2 Click **Sign In,** or create a new Microsoft account if you do not have one.

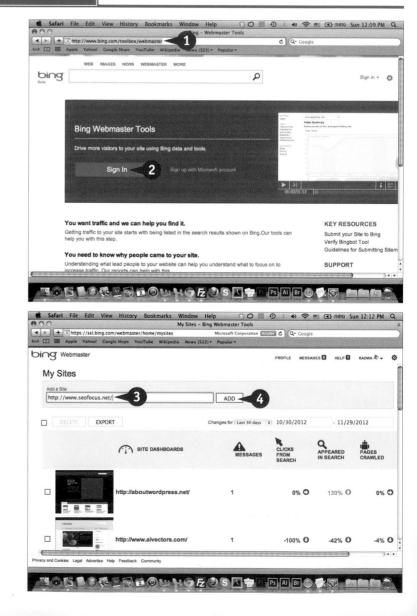

The Bing Webmaster home page appears.

3 Type your website URL.

4 Click **Add.**

The Add a Site page appears.

5 Type your website sitemap path.

6 Click the pop-up menu and select All Day (Default).

7 Click **Add.**

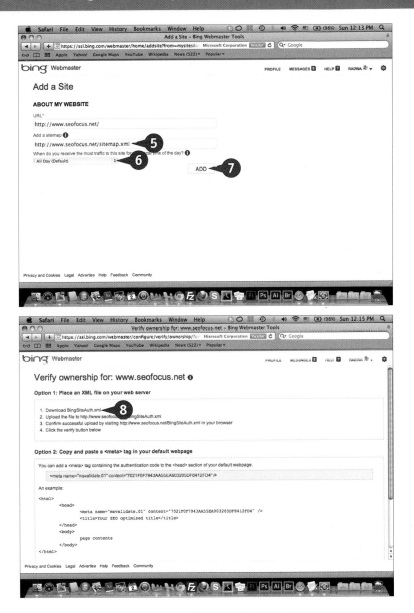

The Verify ownership page appears.

8 Click **BingSiteAuth.xml** to download the site verification file.

TIPS

Can I delete an account from Bing Webmasters?

Yes, you can delete one or more websites from the Bing Webmaster home page. To do so, select the check boxes next to the sites that you would like to delete and click the **Delete** button. You can also export a list of the websites, their verification statuses, and the verification codes.

Can I add multiple users to Bing Webmaster?

Yes, you can add users to Bing Webmaster. Click the **User** link under Configure My Site. You will need to add the new user's e-mail and the user's access level: Read Only, Read/Modify, or Administrator. From this page, you can add multiple sites for the user to access.

continued ▶ 187

Submit a Website to the Bing Webmaster

Verifying your website is essential in the submission process, because it establishes the owner of the website. Only the owner and users added by the owner can display the website's webmaster information or modify it. If you did not verify your website, you will receive an alert stating your website is not verified, and you need to verify its ownership. You can set the default verification method by uploading the verification XML file to your server and clicking Verify. You can always verify your website from the website dashboard by clicking Verify Ownership from the Configure My Site menu.

Submit a Website to the Bing Webmaster (continued)

Note: You can use an FTP application, such as FireFTP, to upload the BingSiteAuth.xml to the server root folder by clicking the **FireFTP** application to open and login to the website FTP account.

⑨ Click **BingSiteAuth.xml** and drag to the website root folder in the server using the FTP application.

Note: You have to sign in to the server FTP to navigate to the root folder.

After the file is uploaded, you can confirm by visiting its path using the browser.

⑩ Type **www.seofocus.net/ BingSiteAuth.xml** in your browser and press **Enter** to confirm the upload.

After confirming www. seofocus.net/BingSiteAuth. xml, close the web page and return to the Verify ownership page in Bing Webmaster tool.

11 Click **Verify.**

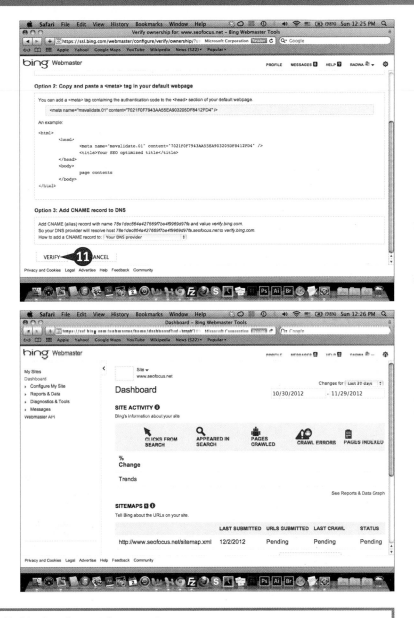

The website is verified and the website Dashboard page appears.

TIP

What other verification options are available in Bing Webmaster?
In addition to uploading the BingSiteAuth.xml file to your server, you can copy a Metadata line <meta name="msvalidate.01" content="7021F0F7943AA55EA903205DF8412FD4" /> and paste it after the opening of the <head> tag in the website home page HTML file. Another option is to add a CNAME (Canonical Name) to the website DNS (Domain Name System) to verify your ownership. The CNAME lets you add multiple services to your domain name IP (Internet Protocol), and the CNAME values to the domain name DNS. The latter option can be complicated and requires advanced skills.

Use the Bing SEO Analyzer

In the Diagnostics & Tools section, Bing provides a number of useful tools that can help you explore your website and optimize it. For example, Keyword Research allows you to explore the website keywords, and Markup Validation checks your website code for errors. Additionally, SEO Analyzer shows you how your website home page or internal pages are optimized for Bing search engine. It shows the errors appearing in your websites, so you can fix them, along with a preview of the website. You can also use SEO Analyzer recommendations to optimize your website for better indexing.

Use the Bing SEO Analyzer

1 Click the website name on the Bing Webmaster home page.

The website's Dashboard page appears.

2 Click **Diagnostics & Tools** under the Dashboard section.

3 Click **SEO Analyzer.**

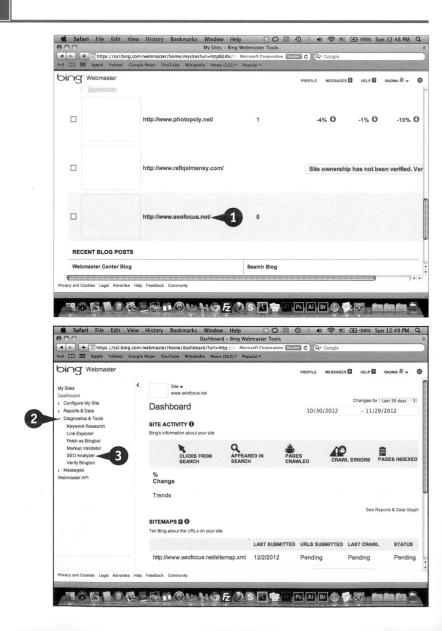

The SEO Analyzer page
appears.

4 Type your website URL.

5 Click **Analyze.**

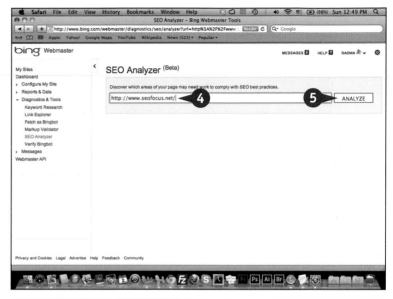

The website analysis results
appear.

TIPS

How does the Keyword Research tool work?
In Bing Webmaster, you can analyze how your
website appears in search results when a user types
a specific keyword in the Bing search field. By using
the Keyword Research tool, you can type the
keyword and other information. The results show
how many times your website appeared in the
search results.

What is the Verify Bingbot?
When search engine crawlers visit your website,
they use different Internet Protocol numbers. While
you might block specific IPs from visiting your
website, you do not want to block any search
engine crawler IPs. This tool allows you to
determine whether the IP is related to Bingbot
by typing the IP and clicking **Submit.**

CHAPTER 10

Working with Social Media and SEO

Social media marketing is closely related to search engine optimization. Although it does not impact the search engine directly, it can help your website receive more traffic via social networks.

Understanding Social Media Marketing

Social media has become an essential part of most Internet users' daily routines. Users find friends, communities, and information on different networking platforms, such as Facebook and Twitter. You can use these social networks to increase traffic to your website and enhance its visibility. Further, social network followers can help build links to your website by sharing links among friends or linking directly to your website. Understanding the social media market and how to engage with website followers can help you gather more followers and expose your website to a larger audience.

Build a Professional Profile

The first step that you need to take is to build a professional profile. The social media profile is your springboard to starting your website promotion. When audiences see that you have a professional profile with useful updates, they will likely follow your page on Facebook, Google Plus, and Twitter. When you build your website profile on social networks, make sure to include accurate descriptions and information about your website, including the important keywords.

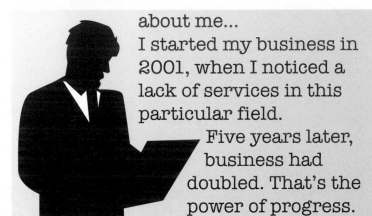

about me...
I started my business in 2001, when I noticed a lack of services in this particular field.
Five years later, business had doubled. That's the power of progress.

Understand Your Audience

Each niche in the market has its particular audience and special characteristics. To increase the exposure of your business profile, you need to understand what type of followers you have and their needs. For example, if you provide training materials and your audience is mostly students, you would add instructional updates, tips, and challenging questions. Also, recognizing your audience can help you identify the best social website to start with to promote your business.

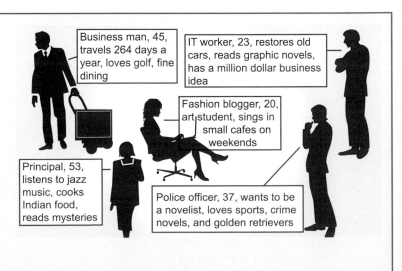

Business man, 45, travels 264 days a year, loves golf, fine dining

IT worker, 23, restores old cars, reads graphic novels, has a million dollar business idea

Fashion blogger, 20, art student, sings in small cafes on weekends

Principal, 53, listens to jazz music, cooks Indian food, reads mysteries

Police officer, 37, wants to be a novelist, loves sports, crime novels, and golden retrievers

Use Personal Language

One of the important issues to consider when posting in social networks is using personal language and communicating with your audience with a direct tone. Personal, friendly language suits social media audiences and encourages followers to respond to your updates using social networking tools such as Like and Share. However, you need to avoid using a casual tone that may not suit some audiences, especially ones in different countries.

Consider Frequent Updates

The frequency of your updates refers to how often you post on a social network page or profile. It is very important to keep the audience engaged with regular updates, which can vary from several updates per day to several updates per week. Too many updates can have a negative impact because it may annoy your audience and turn out to be spam-like messages. Making one to four updates during the day is a safe number that ensures good exposure.

Posted by The Booklover on January 02, 2013   Posted by The Booklover on
y 28, 2013   Posted by The Booklover on January 31, 2013
Posted by The Booklover on February 14, 2013   Posted by The Booklover on February 28,
Posted by The Booklover on March 01, 2013
Posted by The Booklover on March 09, 2013
Posted by The Booklover on March 13, 2013

Build an Engagement Strategy

Strategy is very important in social media marketing and it can help you gain more exposure in social networks. An engagement strategy includes building continuous interaction with your audience using content that you can run directly through social networks such as Facebook and Twitter. Further, you can ask followers questions and build discussion threads. Continually interacting with your followers helps promote your page or profile because the friends of your followers will see their updates and shares about your page.

Use Different Media

While text content is the king in SEO, images and video can increase the number of followers of your business page or profile significantly. Each social network website has specific media users can interact with. For example, Twitter depends mainly on text updates while Facebook uses image and video shares. Further, social media sites such as Pinterest depend mainly on images.

Create a Facebook Page for Your Business

The Facebook page becomes one of the most important tools for social media promotion. You can use it to promote your business, interact with clients, or drive followers and traffic to your website. Facebook pages are indexed by search engines and appear when the search user searches for related keywords. You can use a Facebook page to get better rankings for your website. To create a Facebook page, you will need a Facebook profile, which allows you to create as many pages as you want. On your page, you can add your website logo, introduction, and contact information.

Create a Facebook Page for Your Business

Note: To follow this task, you must sign in to your Facebook account, or create a new account at www.facebook.com if you do not have one.

1. Type **www.facebook.com** in your web browser and press **Enter**.

2. Type your login credentials and click **Log In.**

Your Facebook page appears.

3. Click **Create a Page.**

The Create a Page category appears.

4 Click to choose a business category, for example, Entertainment.

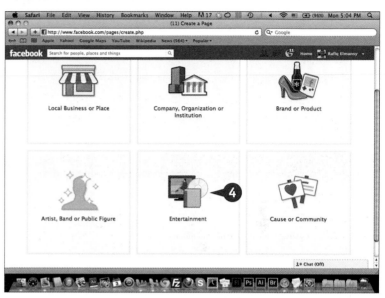

The Business category expands.

5 Click the **Category** pop-up menu and select a specific business category.

6 Type a name for your business website.

7 Review the terms and agreement and then click the **I agree to Facebook Pages Terms** option (☐ changes to ☑).

8 Click **Get Started.**

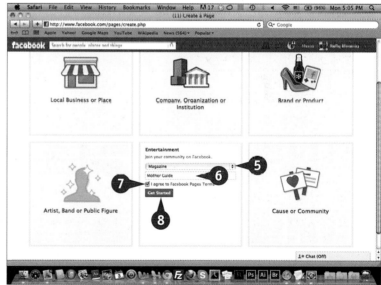

TIP

What is the difference between pages and groups?
You can use Facebook pages for business purposes, such as building a business profile for your company, magazine, or website. In pages, you allow page followers to post on the page timeline. This gives you full responsibility for updates on your Facebook page. On the other hand, the Facebook groups are designed for public discussion and sharing information among an entire group. In most groups, anyone can post an update and news directly to the group, similar to the group's owner. The difference between a member and the group owner is that the owner has administrative privileges, such as the authority to delete updates and ban users.

continued ▶ **197**

Create a Facebook Page for Your Business
(continued)

To increase exposure for your Facebook business page, you can invite followers of your personal page to join the page. You can share business updates on your personal page. You can also create advertisements on your personal page to promote your business page. Facebook provides comprehensive forms for creating ad banners that target website niches and audiences. You can *Pay Per Click* (PPC), pay per impression, which means that your payment model is based on every 1,000 times the advertisement appears to the viewer. This is known as *Cost Per Mille* (CPM).

Create a Facebook Page for Your Business (continued)

The Set Up page appears.

9 Click **Upload From Computer** to upload a photograph from your computer.

Note: Your steps may vary depending on the device you are using.

Note: You can use this step to add a logo later in the process.

The graphic appears.

10 Click **Next** to continue.

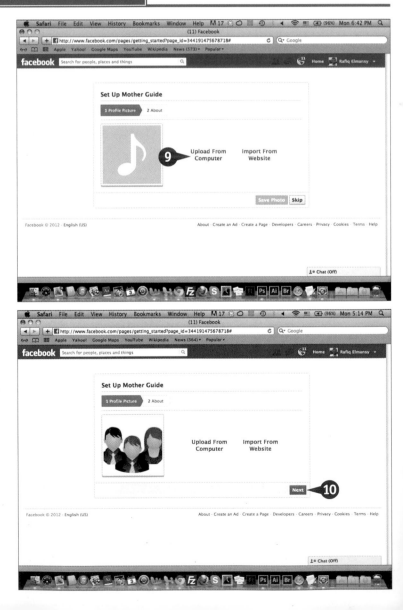

11 Type your website description.

12 Type your main external website URL.

13 Click the **No** option, if this page does not represent a real person, book/magazine, or venue (○ changes to ⊙).

14 Click **Save Info.**

The Facebook business page appears.

Why does the Facebook page name not appear in the URL?

You must have 20 followers to request the page name as the URL. After your page reaches 20 followers, go to **www.facebook.com/username**, select the Facebook page from a list, and choose a name for it. This name has to be available for you to be able to use it.

Can I add administrators to the page?

Yes, you can add administrators to a Facebook business page by clicking the **Edit Page** pop-up menu and then clicking **Admin Roles.** Then type the admin Facebook usernames and set their roles. This is a useful feature if you are running an SEO campaign and need a social media expert to manage one or more pages for your clients.

Create a Google Plus Business Page

Google Plus started as a social network similar to Facebook. Although the number of Google Plus users is still less than Facebook users, it is one of the important social network sites on the Internet that allows users to build business profiles and pages. The big advantage of having an active page on Google Plus is that it integrates with Google search. For example, when you search for specific information, the results from your Google Plus network appear at the top. This can increase your website ranking as well as its traffic.

Create a Google Plus Business Page

Note: To follow this task, you must sign in to your Google account, or create a new account at https://plus.google.com if do not have one.

1 Type **https://plus.google.com** in your web browser and press **Enter**.

2 Type your login credentials and click **Sign In.**

Your Google Plus profile appears.

3 Position your mouse pointer over **More.**

The More menu appears.

④ Click **Pages.**

The Google Plus pages appear.

⑤ Click **Create New Page.**

How can I add a Google Plus button to my website?

The Google Plus button is a small button that you add to any page in your website. Users can click it to join your Google Plus page directly without having to visit it through the browser. To add the Google Plus button, you need to copy specific code and paste it any place in your website HTML code. You can get this code from https://developers.google.com/+/plugins/+1button/?hl=en. You can also customize the size and width of the button.

continued ►

Create a Google Plus Business Page (continued)

Unlike Facebook, Google Plus followers are arranged in circles. You can add followers with similar interests to the same circles. This can help you build and arrange followers' circles. As your number of followers grows, your page will earn higher rankings in the search engine because each search user can see links for you from your followers' shares. Also, building a professional and complete profile can help you increase the number of followers. The links in Google Plus can help you direct links back to your website, which improves your ranking.

Create a Google Plus Business Page (continued)

The Create New Page main categories appear.

6 Click to choose a business category; for example, Arts, Entertainment or Sports.

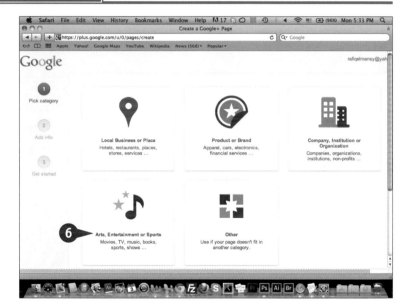

The Business categories expand.

7 Click the **Select a category** pop-up menu and select the type of page you want to build; for example, Blog.

8 Click **Next** to continue.

The Create a Google+ page form appears.

9 Type a name for your business website.

10 Type your main external website URL.

11 Click the **content appropriate** pop-up menu and make a selection.

12 Click the **I agree to the Pages Terms and I am authorized to create this page** option (☐ changes to ☑).

13 Click **Continue.**

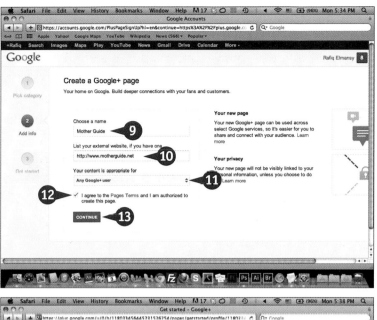

The Google Plus page setup appears.

14 Click **Add your cover photo** to add your photo to your cover page.

15 Click **Add your logo** to add your logo to your page.

16 Type a description of your page.

17 Type your page contact information.

18 Click **Finish.**

Your Google Plus business page appears.

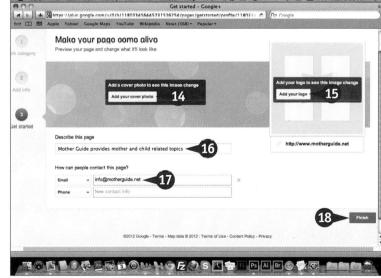

TIP

How can I build an interactive Google Plus account?
Building an interactive Google Plus account can help you promote your website content and earn your links better rankings when followers share them or like them by clicking the Google Plus button. The best way to facilitate strong interaction is to share various useful links from your friends' shares and comments with others along with positive comments. This encourages others to like your posts and share your links, bringing potential visitors to your website and subsequently helping increase your website's ranking.

Create a Twitter Account for Your Website

Twitter is another important social media tool that allows you to send updates or tweets up to 140 characters in length to your followers. Twitter followers can retweet or share website updates to their followers to increase the exposure of your tweets that refer to Twitter updates. While Twitter does not directly impact SEO, it can help increase traffic to your website, especially when you have a strong followers for your website. Unlike with Facebook or Google+, you cannot build pages in Twitter. Your main profile is your business page and you have to create an account for each website.

Create a Twitter Account for Your Website

1. Type **www.twitter.com** in your web browser and press **Enter**.

   The Twitter Sign In and Sign Up page appears.

2. Type your website or business name.

3. Type your website e-mail address; for example, *info@motherguide.net*.

4. Type a password.

5. Click **Sign up for Twitter.**

   The Twitter sign-up form appears.

6. Type your desired Twitter name.

7. Click **Create my account.**

The Twitter account home page appears.

8 Click **Next.**

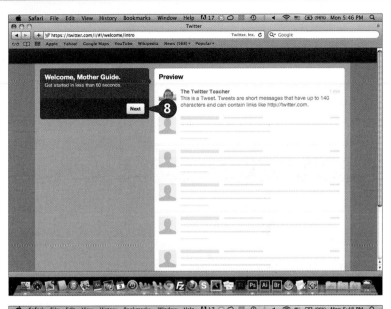

9 Click **Follow** on five separate accounts to help build your timeline and receive Tweets.

10 Click **Next.**

TIPS

What is the hashtag?
The hashtag (#) is a sign that you add to important keywords in a Twitter update. You can also use a hashtag to add specific keywords at the end of your message; for example, (#photography). Adding a hashtag to keywords helps categorize your messages and enables other users to easily find your messages by using the Twitter search.

What are mentions?
Mentions refer to adding a specific Twitter username in the body of the message in the format @username. This mention appears in the other user's timeline. The mentions are important in social media because you can use them to communicate directly with your followers, even if you are not following them.

Create a Twitter Account for Your Website

(continued)

Building a sustainable Twitter profile for your business can greatly improve your website traffic. You should provide information, links, and services that your audiences need. This will drive followers to your website and they will share the links. You also need to start conversations or discussions with your followers. It does not matter how many followers you have; most important is having followers who are interested in your website niche and interact with your account.

Create a Twitter Account for Your Website (continued)

⓫ Click **Following** on five people that you want to follow.

⓬ Click **Next.**

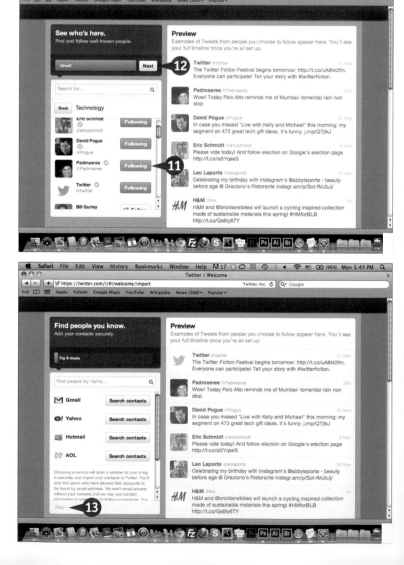

The Search contacts by e-mail page appears.

⓭ Click **Skip.**

The Add character page appears.

⑭ Click **Upload image** to upload a website logo from your computer.

⑮ Type your website description and URL.

⑯ Click **Done.**

Your website Twitter home page appears.

How to add a Twitter button to my website?
The Twitter button allows your website visitors to tweet about your website or its new updates directly from the web page, which helps increase the number of website followers. To add the button, you first need to get the code for it from http://twitter.com/about/resources/buttons#tweet; then paste the button code into your website HTML code. Twitter allows you to customize the button size and style. Also, you can set up the button to use the exact URL or the current web page. The button can show the tweet count and the custom text that appears before the tweeted URL. You can also customize the button to display a specific recommended Twitter account, add the website's Twitter account, and add a hashtag for search purposes.

Manage Social Accounts Using HootSuite

The increasing number of social media websites makes it harder for social media experts to manage all their social accounts, especially when social media is only one part of the entire SEO process. Thus, there are multiple third-party applications that help you handle all your accounts easily from one place. Some of these applications are desktop-based and others are web-based. The HootSuite application provides comprehensive features for managing social accounts from Facebook, Twitter, and LinkedIn. The free package allows you to have up to five free social accounts.

Manage Social Accounts Using HootSuite

Add a Social Media Account

Note: To follow this task, you must sign in to your HootSuite account, or create a new account at www.hootsuite.com if do not have one.

① Type **www.hootsuite.com** in your web browser and press **Enter**.

② Type your login credentials and click **Secure Login.**

Note: You must sign into the social media network to add the network.

The Getting Started page appears.

③ Click **Add a *Twitter* profile**, or replace *Twitter* with the social media network of your choice.

The Add Social Network page appears.

④ Click **Connect with *Twitter*,** or the social media network of your choice.

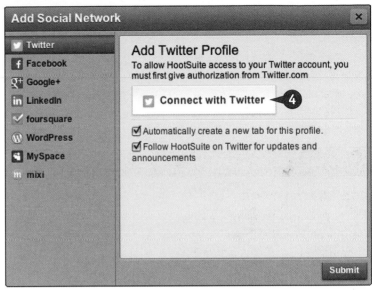

The Twitter/Authorize an application page appears.

⑤ Type your Twitter account name.

⑥ Type your Twitter account password.

⑦ Click **Authorize app.**

Your Twitter updates appear in the Hootsuite Twitter tab on the home page.

TIPS

Where do new accounts appear?
New accounts appear as a new tab in the HootSuite Streams section and display your followers' updates, messages, and mentions. You can also click your profile name in the left floating menu to see added accounts. All accounts appear under the My Social Networks section.

What social networks are supported in HootSuite?
HootSuite supports adding accounts from Twitter, Facebook, Google Plus, LinkedIn, foursquare, WordPress, MySpace, and mixi. When you add an account, it appears as a separate tab in the HootSuite Stream, so you can check updates for each account individually.

continued ▶

In addition to managing accounts, HootSuite lets you schedule automatic posts to one or more of your social accounts. This is useful when you are not able to access your account or are busy during a given time. You can add the posts and schedule them to be published on specific dates or let HootSuite automatically set a time to publish them. The scheduled posts appear under the Scheduled link, which you access by clicking Publisher in the left menu.

Manage Social Accounts Using HootSuite (continued)

Schedule a Social Update

1 Click the **Compose message** area on the HootSuite dashboard after you sign in.

The message composer opens.

2 Type your message.

3 Click the **Scheduling** button (📅).

The Schedule message dialog box appears.

④ Click a desired schedule date.

⑤ Click the time pop-up menus and set a time.

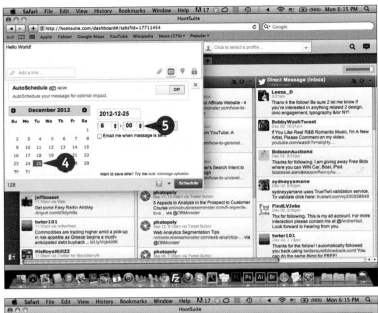

⑥ Click the **Account list** button (🔄) and select the accounts.

⑦ Click **Schedule**.

Your message is scheduled for publishing on the specified date.

TIPS

How can I delete an account?
You can delete an account from your profile name on the left menu. This opens the profile page with a list of the accounts. When you click the icon next to each account, it displays the functions drop-down list. Then, click the **Remove from HootSuite** link to remove the account. You can add it later or add other accounts using the **Add a Social Network** link on the same page.

What is the HootSuite Analytics?
You can find statistics about your posts in the Analytics link in the left menu. You can create statistics for Facebook or Google Analytics. These reports can give you information about how your social marketing plan affects your website SEO.

Work with Social Bookmarking Sites

Social bookmarking websites are sites where you can submit bookmarks for your favorite links and share them with your friends and groups on the sites. When you do this, it can increase your website backlinks, especially when the link is shared among many of your friends on these bookmarking sites. One famous social bookmarking site is Delicious at https://delicious.com. You can create an account on the Delicious website and start adding your favorite links and your website's links to increase its backlinks.

Work with Social Bookmarking Sites

Note: Log in to your http://delicious.com account, or create a new one to see this link.

1. Click **Add link** in your Delicious profile.

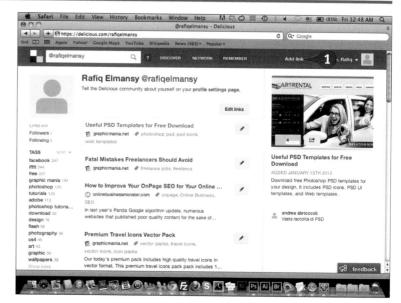

The Add a new link dialog box appears.

2. Type the URL for the site you would like to submit.

3. Click **Add link.**

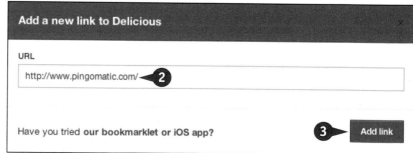

The link information box appears.

4 Fill in the form.

5 Click **Add link.**

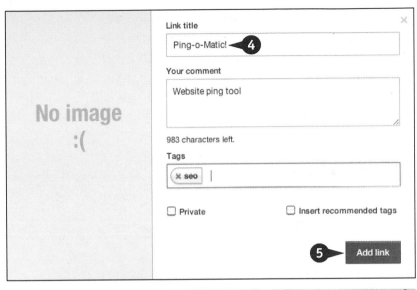

The link is added to your profile.

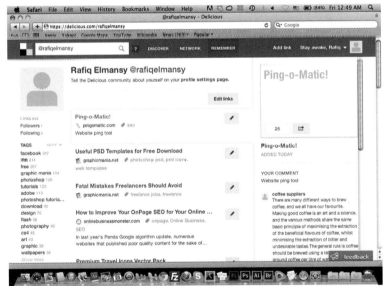

How to get traffic from Delicious?
You can use Delicious to drive traffic and backlinks to your website by increasing the number of shares for your site's links. You can do this by becoming an active member in Delicious, building a strong friends base, and submitting high-quality links and shares. Interacting with friends and sharing their links can help you to build a strong profile that you can use to reach a larger audience and get your friends to share your links in return. While this process takes time, it increases the number of backlinks to your website considerably as well its traffic.

CHAPTER 11

Working with AdWords

Google AdWords allows you to create advertisements on Google partner websites and Google search result pages, known as paid search. AdWords helps your website receive targeted traffic from Google Search and increase your potential traffic and ranking through the impact that these ads have on your website. AdWords ads can help you achieve search engine optimization (SEO) results much faster and more easily.

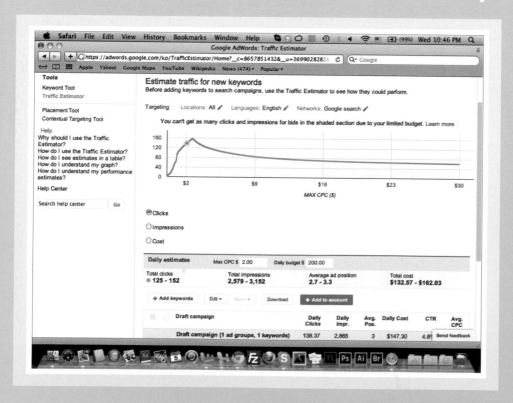

Create an AdWords Campaign

When you first use AdWords, you create an AdWords campaign where you can display ads in Google Search, partner sites, or both. You also set up the target device such as desktop or mobile devices and the location where you want the ad to display. Each campaign requires you to set up the default Cost Per Click (CPC) bid for the first ad in the campaign and the daily budget that you plan to spend on advertising per day. Each campaign can include one or more ads in different formats, such as text and images, that is known as ad groups.

Create an AdWords Campaign

1 Type **https://adwords. google.com** in your web browser.

The Google AdWords page opens.

2 Type your e-mail address.

3 Type your password.

4 Click **Sign In**.

Note: If you do not have a Google Account, click **Start Now** to create a new account.

The Google AdWords home page appears.

5 Click **Campaigns.**

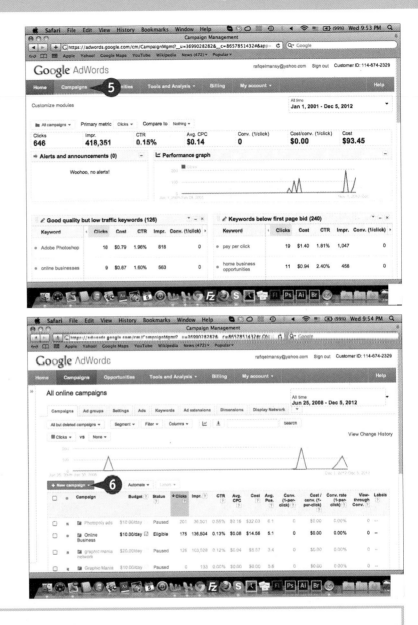

The Campaigns page appears.

6 Click **+ New campaign.**

TIP

How does Pay Per Click (PPC) work?

Pay Per Click (PPC) refers to the advertising networks' charge per user click. As an advertiser, you pay a specific amount of money for each click on your banner or link. The price for each ad depends on the keywords that the ad targets. The high ad position in the search engine results page is determined based on your bid price and your ad quality score, which refers to the ad relativity to the user search query. If you submit a high bid for specific keyword and your ad gets a high quality score, then your ad can appear in the top of the search engine results page, unlike the other ads with low bid price or low quality and relativity score.

continued ▶

Create an AdWords Campaign (continued)

The AdWords campaign settings that you apply when creating the campaign are global, meaning that they apply to all the ad groups or ads created under the campaign. For example, if you set the company target to the United States, all the ad groups located under this campaign are targeted to the United States. Also, the budget that you assign for the campaign will be allocated to all the ads inside this campaign. You can use your campaign to arrange your ads and manage it more efficiently. For example, you can add a campaign for a specific website or marketing plan.

Create an AdWords Campaign (continued)

The New campaign pop-up menu appears.

7 Click **Search Network only**.

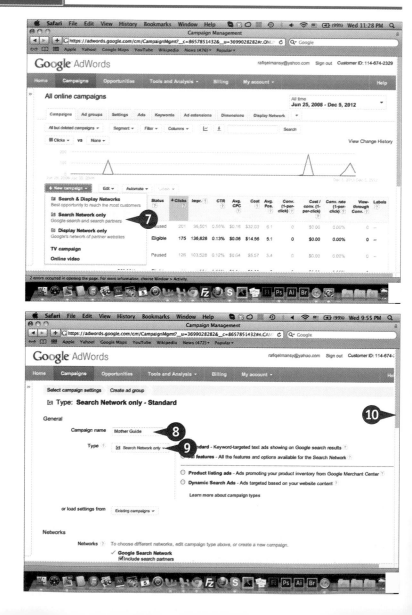

The New campaign form appears.

8 Type your website campaign name in the Campaign name field; for example, Mother Guide.

9 Click the **Type** menu and select Search Network **only** from the list.

10 Scroll down the page.

More form options appear.

11 Click a **Network** option
(☐ changes to ☑).

12 Click a **Device** option
(○ changes to ◉).

13 Click a **Location** option
(○ changes to ◉).

14 Scroll down the page.

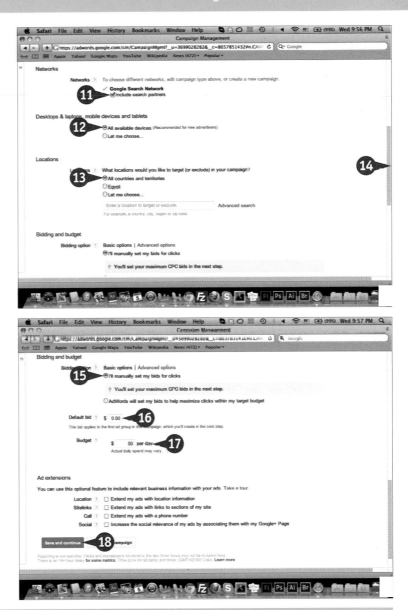

More form options appear.

15 Click the **I'll manually set
my bids for clicks** option
(○ changes to ◉).

16 Type a dollar amount in the
Default bid field.

17 Type a dollar amount in the
Budget field.

18 Click **Save and continue.**

You may continue by setting
up the payment method.

TIPS

Why does the campaign setting call for creating an ad group?

By default, Google asks you to create an ad group after you set up the campaign. After you click **Save and continue**, the new campaign appears in the campaigns list on the left side of the screen. Click **Cancel creating ad group** to create an empty campaign and then add the ad groups later.

Can I copy settings from another campaign?

When working with different campaigns targeting similar locations and having similar budgets, you do not have to add your settings again. You can import settings from another existing campaign using the General section in the new campaign form. Choose the name of the campaign from the **Load setting from** list.

Create an Ad Group

You can create the ad group while you are setting up the AdWords campaign or from the campaign page clicking the **+ New ad group** button. The ad group content, such as title, text, and images, has to represent the product or service and compel viewers to click on it. It is very important to use the targeted keywords in the ad group because this may increase the clicks on the ad. Also, using clear, concise language helps deliver the ad message to the audience. There are different types of ad groups, such as text, image, mobile, product list, and more.

Create an Ad Group

1 Click **Campaigns** on the Google AdWords home page.

The Campaign section appears.

2 Click a campaign.

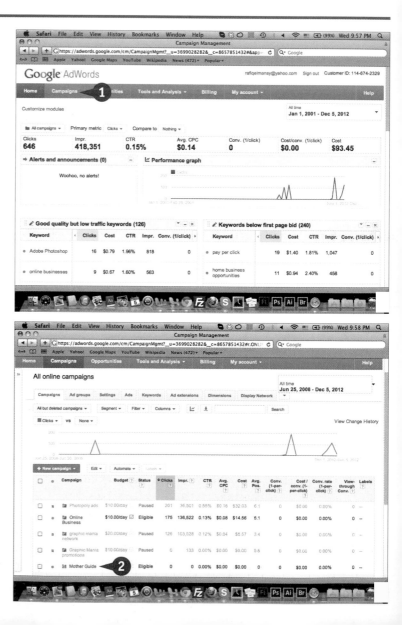

The campaign page appears.

3 Click **+ New ad group.**

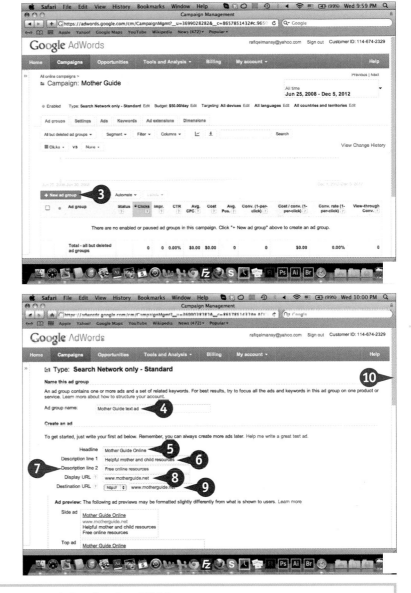

The New Ad group page appears.

4 Type your ad group name using keywords.

5 Type a headline for your ad.

6 Type a description for your ad.

7 Type another description for your ad.

8 Type your display URL.

9 Type your destination URL.

10 Scroll down the page.

TIP

What is the different between a display URL and destination URL?
When you create the ad group, you add the URL for the website that you would like to advertise. There are two types of URLs that you add when you are setting the ad zone. The first type is the display URL, which is the site link that appears to the ad viewer. The second type is the destination URL that is the actual link that the user visits after clicking the ad banner title. Both URLs can be different from each other. For example, the destination link can be too long to appear in an ad banner. You can add the main domain URL in the display URL and the long link in the destination URL. This can help the user to remember your domain instead of writing a long, complex URL. In addition, note that a display URL has a character limit.

continued ▶ **221**

Create an Ad Group (continued)

After you set an ad group click price bid, Google helps you to determine the estimated bid for your keywords. If your bid is higher than the estimate, this does not affect the estimate and you will find that the cost is lower than your setup. If the keyword Cost Per Click (CPC) is lower than the estimated price, your ad will not appear in a competitive position in the Search Network or the Display Network. Choosing the right keywords and estimated bids are very important to maximize the exposure of the ad group.

Create an Ad Group (continued)

The Keywords section appears.

11 Type the keywords related to the ad group.

12 Click to add related keyword suggestions from the list.

13 Scroll down the page.

The ad group bids appear.

14 Type your ad group bid.

15 Click **Estimate search traffic.**

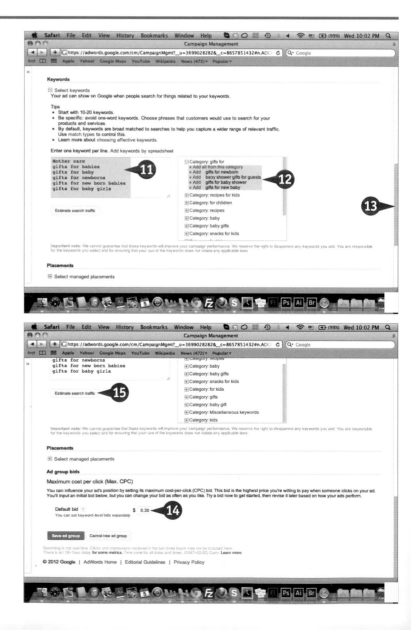

The estimated CPC, expected clicks, and daily cost appear.

16 Click **Save ad group.**

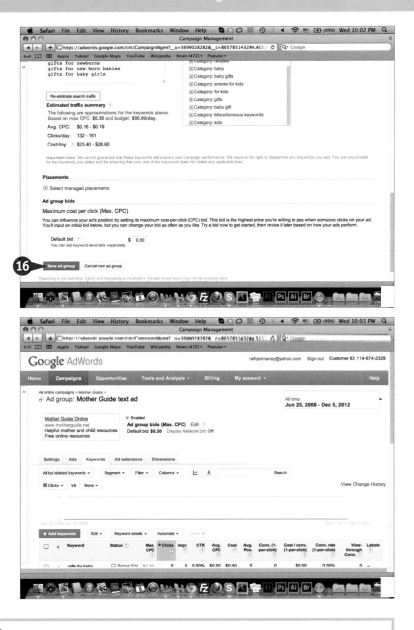

The ad group appears in the campaign list.

TIP

What are the different ad group types?

You can create multiple types of ad groups. Most common are text ads and image ads, where you upload a standard size image and use it instead of a text ad. Image ads are only available in campaigns that support the Display Network. The Specialized search ad lets you target Google images and YouTube videos. This type is useful for targeting clients who depend on images and video in their search. The WAP (Wireless Application Protocol) mobile ad targets mobile devices, such as iPhones, and technology. The Product listing ad helps you promote a product, and the Dynamic search ad displays an ad based on the website content.

Using the Keyword Tool

The Keyword tool is one of the essential features that can help SEO experts find the rank of keywords and understand its search volume, which indicates how many users type these keywords in the search query. Understanding search volume for specific keyword can help you to know which keyword you should optimize in the website content and the best combination of keywords to use. In order to search for specific keyword rank, you need to add one or more keywords to the words area, the URL, and category. You can also set the target location, language, and devices.

Using the Keyword Tool

1 Click the **Tools and Analysis** menu on the Google AdWords home page.

The Tools and Analysis drop-down menu appears.

2 Click **Keyword Tool.**

The Keyword Tool page appears.

3 Type one or more keywords in the Word or phrase field.

4 Click **Search.**

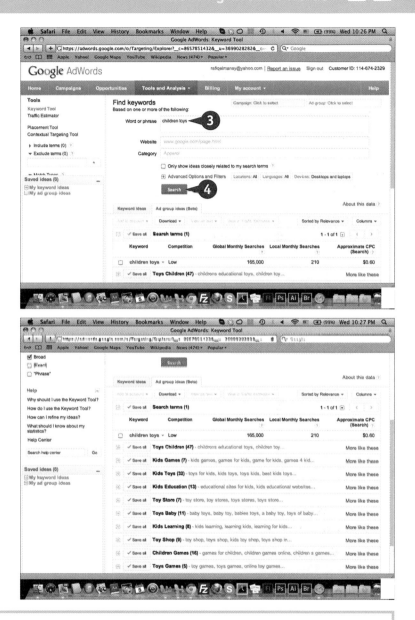

The search volume, competition, and CPC for this keyword and related keywords appear.

How do I use the Keyword Tool in SEO?
When you are creating content for your website or optimizing it for search engines, you have to choose the best keyword or group of keywords to focus on to help improve your website's rank in the search engine results page (SERP). The Keyword Tool can give you an idea about the best keywords to use in your website. The high search volume means that there are many users who search for this keyword on Google. The competition level refers to the number of advertisers that bid on the keyword in AdWords. The Keyword Tool can give you ideas about other similar keywords that you can add to your website to increase its search engine ranking.

Using the Traffic Estimator Tool

The Traffic Estimator tool lets you calculate the estimated clicks that you will receive when users click a specific keyword or group of keywords. This feature can help you get a better understanding of the traffic that you may receive from your AdWords campaign. It can give you an idea about a keyword's cost, which can enable you to focus on the keywords that produce a high volume of clicks for a relatively low cost. You can either add your keywords by typing them in the Traffic Estimator field or import them from an Excel CSV document.

Using the Traffic Estimator Tool

1 Click the **Tools and Analysis** menu on the Google AdWords home page.

The Tools and Analysis drop-down menu appears.

2 Click **Traffic Estimator.**

The Traffic Estimator page appears.

3 Type a keyword in the keyword field.

4 Click **Get estimates.**

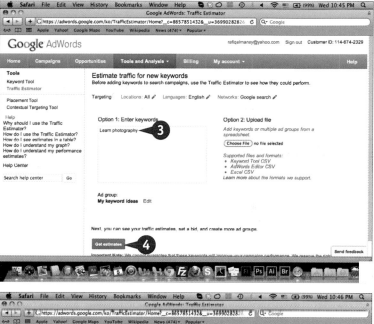

The Estimate graph appears.

5 Type a dollar amount in the Max CPC $ field.

6 Type a dollar amount in the Daily budget $ field.

The estimated daily clicks and the average cost appear.

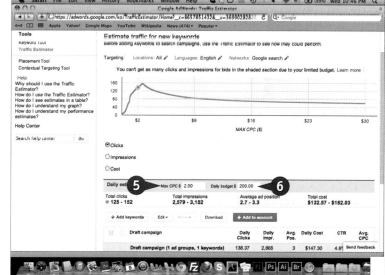

How do I set up the Traffic Estimator tool?
You can set up the Traffic Estimator to get accurate ad placement analyses. You can also use it to test the impact of keywords on users with specific criteria. In the Traffic Estimator page, you set the location, language, and Google network that will display the ad. The cost and budget results will be more accurate than the general data.

What is the Ad Preview and Diagnosis tool in AdWords?
The Ad Preview and Diagnosis tool allows you to see how your ad looks in other websites and Display Networks. To preview your ad, type the keyword in the Preview field and select the Google search domain, language, location, and device.

Using the Contextual Targeting Tool

The Contextual Targeting Tool is another comprehensive tool in AdWords, and it allows you to search for specific keywords and display all the groups of keywords related to the entered term. You can save these groups to use in AdWords campaigns. You can also check some of the websites that will include these keywords using Google Display Network or AdSense advertisements. In addition, it can give you suggested bids you can use them in your AdWords campaign or to optimize your website content in more advanced ways.

Using the Contextual Targeting Tool

1 Click the **Tools and Analysis** menu on the Google AdWords home.

The Tools and Analysis drop-down menu appears.

2 Click **Contextual Targeting Tool.**

The Contextual Targeting Tool page appears.

3 Type a keyword in the Tools field.

4 Click **Search.**

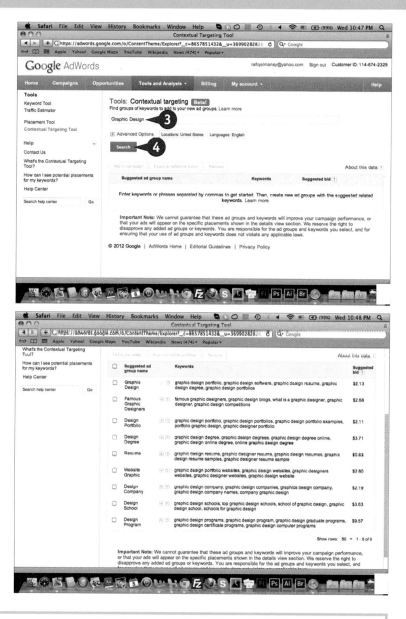

The Suggested ad group name and Keywords appear.

How do I view where the keywords will appear?
The Contextual Targeting Tool lets you view where your keywords will appear by providing examples of Display Network websites. When you search for keywords that are related to your website, it can show you competitor websites related to a particular keyword and help you analyze them. After the suggested ad group names and keywords appear, you can click the View Predicted Placement icon to display a long list of the websites that can host these keywords as part of their Display Network ads. You can also click the plus (+) icon next to each website to display the web pages that will display this keyword.

Work with Analyze Competitions

The Analyze Competitions feature in the Google AdWords Opportunities section lets you see how your AdWords ad campaign is performing compared with other advertisers in the same category or business niche. You can compare your campaign based on many factors, such as the number of impressions and clicks; the Average position (Avg Position); and the Click-Through-Rate (CTR), which shows the number of clicks a campaign's link receives. You can use this feature to measure the success of your ad campaign. To see this information you have to have active campaigns or previous campaign data in your AdWords account.

Work with Analyze Competitions

1 Click the **Opportunities** tab on the Google AdWords home page.

The Opportunities page appears.

2 Click **Analyze competition.**

The Analyze competition page appears.

③ Click the **Impressions** down arrow (▾) and select Avg Position.

The comparison results appear based on the average position.

How do I view information for competitors?

Google AdWords lets you change the advertising campaign category to get more focused information about your competitors. When, you click a category from the list, information about other related subcategories appear, which can help you determine your competition level for these categories.

CHAPTER 12

Applying SEO to WordPress Blogs

Content Management Systems (CMS) are server-side platforms that allow you to build your website and add content easily using *Graphic User Interface (GUI)* elements such as text editors. WordPress is a commonly used CMS because it is easy to use and search engine friendly. You can use WordPress to create blogs, websites, and simple e-commerce stores.

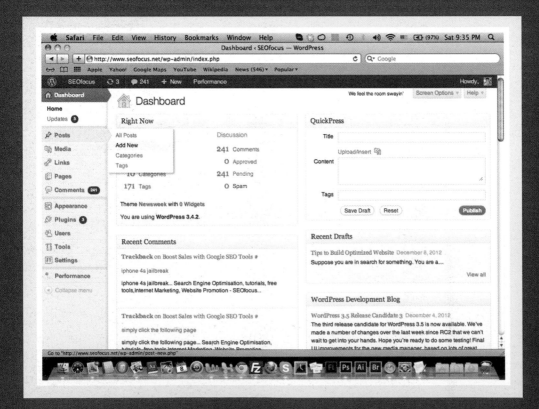

Understanding WordPress CMS

Although WordPress was originally a blogging CMS, it is now used to build corporate websites and e-commerce stores. You can either use www.wordpress.com to build a free blog where you can get free hosting and a blog name or you can install WordPress on your own server by following the steps outlined in this link: http://codex.wordpress.org/Installing_WordPress. Installing WordPress requires that you know how to set up domain names and servers. Each WordPress website has an admin page where you can add content, change the website layout, or add features and functions. WordPress is based on the *PHP (Hypertext Processor)* programming language that is used to create dynamic web pages.

WordPress Themes

The website or blog design in WordPress depends on *themes*. These are groups of images, PHP files, and CSS (Cascading Style Sheets) files used to create the graphical style for the website menus, forms, and other features. You can upload the themes to the server in the folder /wp-content/themes/. To apply the uploaded theme, you activate it from the Themes section in the WordPress admin page. The layout of the website or blog plays an important role in SEO optimization; it has to be clear and ensure that the content loads easily. It can be difficult for search engine spiders to crawl large files. Further, the layout should be user friendly, display the content in the top portion of the page, and have balance between text and images. A wide variety of WordPress themes are available on the web for free as well as for a fee. You can find free themes in the WordPress Directory at www.wordpress.org/extend/themes.

WordPress Plugins

WordPress plugins are a group of PHP-based files that add features and functions to WordPress websites or blogs. Unlike themes, plugins include functions such as contact forms, social media buttons, and more. Different types of plugins can optimize your WordPress website with just a few clicks. There are two methods for installing plugins. The first one is to search for the plugin and install it directly from the Plugins section on the admin page, and the second one is to upload the plugin folder to /wp-content/ themes/ on the WordPress website server, and enable the plugins from the admin page. Use plugins wisely because they include a lot of code, which can make a site slower than normal. You can find a huge number of plugins in WordPress Plugin Directory at http://wordpress.org/extend/plugin.

WordPress and SEO

WordPress is one of the common CMSs that works well with the SEO process. The WordPress site page and archive structure lends itself to optimal content crawling. Also, it is easy to customize each page or post URL to include important keywords for indexing, which are known as *permalinks*. If you choose an SEO-friendly theme, it can aid optimization for your

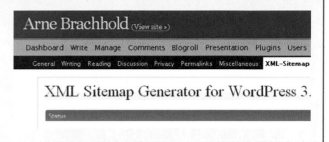

website. WordPress plugins play a significant role in optimizing websites, with an array of different plugins to help you optimize content as well as files. Also, you can customize settings for comments and *pingbacks* to help increase the content optimization. Pingbacks occur when your website links to a specific site and sends updates to the site about the link.

WordPress Content

Content is an essential part of WordPress websites and you need to optimize it in order to appear in search engine results. You can add content to WordPress easily as *posts* or *pages*. Posts are content updates that you can add to your website every day, and they are archived on the blog home page. Pages contain static content that you do not change regularly, such as

contact information and the company information. You can use the text editor in WordPress to format content and headings to meet with SEO guidelines. The content can be arranged in *tags* or *categories*, which are classified for your website content. Tags are keywords that you add to each post and you include the important keywords in each post or page.

WordPress Widgets

WordPress *widgets* are comments sections that you can add to the WordPress sidebar and footer areas. These widgets can include different features, such as recent posts, related posts, ad spaces, and social icons. You can add widgets to either the sidebar or the footer from the Widgets link in the Appearance section on the admin page. In this link, you will find

Related
Akismet Widget
Archives Widget
Author Grid Widget

many widgets that you can drag and drop to available areas in your blog or website. Not only are widgets easy to use, but also you can use them to increase the number of internal links on your home page, which can affect page rank and page views. Also, you can use them to display categories for the website content.

Install the W3 Total Cache Plugin

Website or blog loading speed is an essential factor in SEO. Ample speed can help search engine crawlers index more pages in less time, whereas with slow websites, crawlers may skip slow content. The W3 Total Cache Plugin is one of the plugins that you can install on WordPress and configure to create caches or recorded files from the website on the server. This means the user can access static site information without needing to load it again. This cached version of the website files can help speed content loading and result in a lighter network or bandwidth traffic load.

Install the W3 Total Cache Plugin

1 Type **www.seofocus.net/ wp-admin/** in your web browser and press **Enter**.

The WordPress Log In page appears.

2 Type your username.

3 Type your password.

4 Click **Log In.**

Note: The admin username and password is created when you install WordPress on the server. You may also ask your server administrator to install it.

The WordPress Dashboard
appears.

5 Position your mouse pointer
over **Plugins**.

The Plugins menu appears.

6 Click **Add New** in the pop-up
menu.

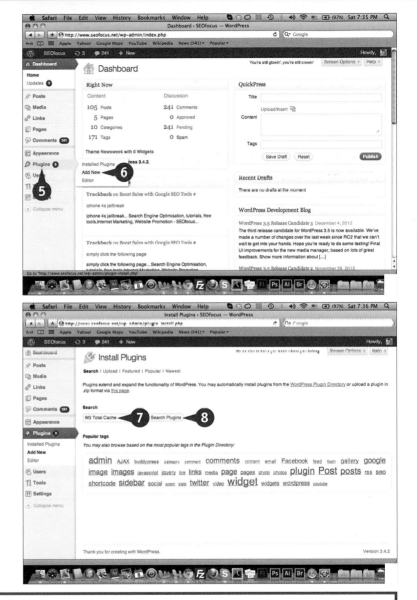

The Install Plugins
page appears.

7 Type **W3 Total Cache.**

8 Click **Search Plugins.**

TIPS

What is caching?
Caching is a method for storing files. The cached
data can be HTML, JavaScript, CSS, and images.
With a cached version of a website, the website
loading speed increases because the server does not
have to generate dynamic files for each user's visit.
Instead, the user views the cached data unless there
is an update to the website.

How can I uninstall a plugin?
You can remove any plugin from your website
through the WordPress admin page. Under the
Plugins section, locate the plugin in the list and
click **Deactivate** to remove it from the website.
Then remove the plugin folder or files from the
server through the FTP client that is used to upload
the website files to the server.

continued ▶ 237

While you can install the W3 Total Cache directly from the WordPress admin page, you can also download it to your computer and upload it directly to the server using any FTP client. You can download the W3 Total Cache from www.wordpress.org/extend/plugins/w3-total-cache. Download the plugin, extract its compressed file, and upload the plugin folder to /wp-content/plugins/. Then, go to Plugins in the admin page and activate the plugin from the new Plugins list. When you install the W3 Total Cache, it creates a number of files and folders in the plugins folder or in the wp-content folder.

Install the W3 Total Cache Plugin (continued)

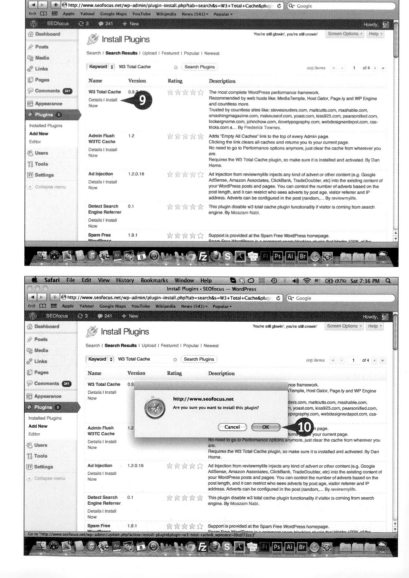

The plugins appear.

9 Click **Install Now** below W3 Total Cache.

An alert message appears.

10 Click **OK.**

The Plugin installation page appears.

⑪ Click **Activate Plugin.**

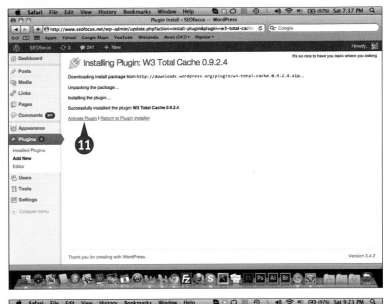

The plugin is activated.

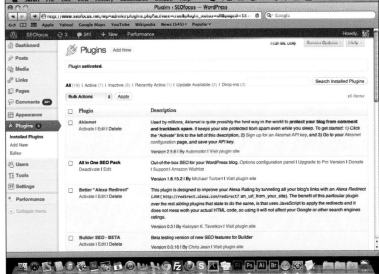

What are alternatives to the W3 Total Cache plugin?
In addition to the W3 Total Cache, there are other caching plugins that you can use to improve your website's loading speed. The WP Super Cache is a common plugin that is simple to use. It is less complex than the W3 Total Cache plugin. However, it has the disadvantage that when you uninstall it, it does not leave remaining files on the server as the W3 Total Cache does. You can download it from the WordPress admin or from http://wordpress.org/extend/plugins/wp-super-cache/. Also, you can use Hyper Cache, which is a new caching plugin that can greatly improve your website's speed. You can download this plugin from http://wordpress.org/extend/plugins/hyper-cache/.

Configure the W3 Total Cache

After installing the W3 Total Cache, it is important to configure it correctly in order to get the most out of it. Configuring the W3 Total Cache lets you set up the server files cache, *minifying* JavaScript and CSS files, which means you make them smaller and faster to load. Also, it allows you to configure the *Content Delivery Network (CDN)* that copies the server files onto servers from various locations so they reach users more quickly. The configuration process is pretty easy; you choose configuration options that allow server file caching.

Configure the W3 Total Cache

1 Position your mouse pointer over **Performance.**

2 Click **General Settings** in the pop-up menu.

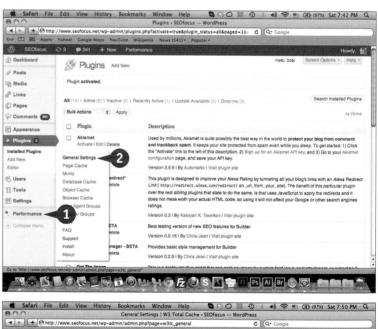

The W3 Total Cache settings appear.

3 Click **Disable** in the General section.

This disables the Preview mode.

4 Scroll down to the Page Cache section.

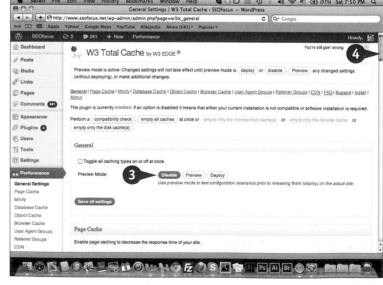

5 In the Page Cache section, click the **Enable** option under the Page Cache section (☐ changes to ☑).

6 Click the **Enable** option under the Minify section (☐ changes to ☑).

7 Click the **Manual** option under the Minify mode (○ changes to ◉).

8 Scroll down to see more Minify settings.

9 Click the **Minify Cache Method** pop-up menu and select Disk.

10 Click the **HTML minifier** pop-up menu and select Default.

11 Click the **JS minified** pop-up menu and select JSMin.

12 Click the **CSS minified** pop-up menu and select Default.

13 Scroll down to the Database Cache section.

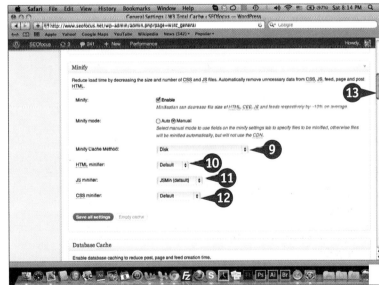

TIP

What is the Content Delivery Network?

The Content Delivery Network (CDN) is a number of distributed servers that are located in different places. These servers are known as *data centers* and are used to multiply data on the Internet. When a user visits a website with CDN service enabled, the CDN delivers the content to the user from the nearest available data center. This can increase the availability of content and website performance, especially for websites that receive a lot of traffic or deliver large-size media files, such as live streaming media, videos, and applications. Usually, the website owner pays for the CDN service based on the bandwidth users request from the CDN data centers.

continued ▶ 241

Configure the W3 Total Cache (continued)

In addition to the general settings in the W3 Total Cache plugin, you can find advanced settings at the top of the plugin settings page. These advanced settings include more options for server performance and handling files on the server. The advanced features include page cache options, minify options, database cache options, browser cache options, and CDN information that you can set by integrating the website with a CDN provider. If you are not familiar with the advanced options, you can simply set the plugins' general information, which is good enough to improve your website performance.

Configure the W3 Total Cache (continued)

14 In the Database Cache section, click the **Enable** option (☐ changes to ☑).

15 Click the **Database Cache Method** pop-up menu and select Disk.

16 Scroll down to the Object Cache section.

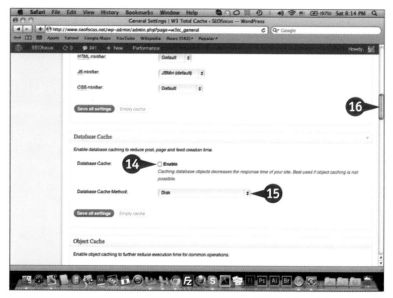

17 In the Object Cache section, click the **Enable** option (☐ changes to ☑).

18 Click the **Object Cache Method** pop-up menu and select Disk.

19 Click the **Enable** option (☐ changes to ☑) under the Browser Cache section.

20 Scroll down to Miscellaneous.

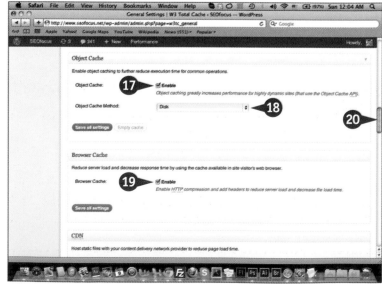

㉑ In the Miscellaneous section, click the **Verify rewrite rules** option (☐ changes to ☑).

㉒ Click to deselect the **Enable file locking** option (☑ changes to ☐).

㉓ Click the **Optimize disk enhanced page and minify caching for NFS** option (☐ changes to ☑).

㉔ Click the **Enable news dashboard widget** option (☐ changes to ☑).

㉕ Click the **Enable Google Page Speed dashboard widget** option (☐ changes to ☑).

㉖ Click **Save All settings**.

The plugin settings are saved.

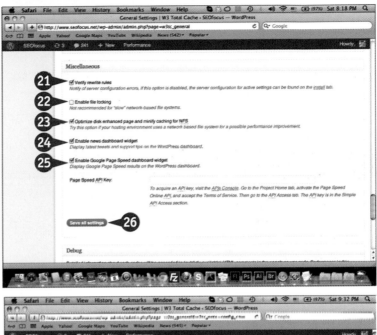

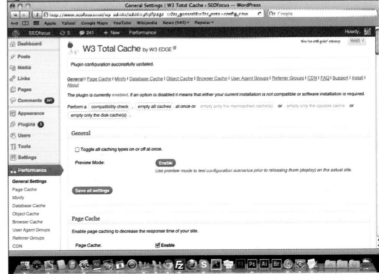

TIP

How do I integrate CDN with W3 Total Cache?
To use the CDN service on your website, use a caching plugin such as W3 Total Cache. You can register your website with the CDN provider to receive an API ID, API Key, and host name. API is the Application programming Interface that is used to link your server with the CDN service. This host name replaces the current path for all your website files. You need to enable the CDN from the W3 Total Cache setting and set it to use the desired CDN services. Then, you can access the CDN settings and add the API information to the required fields.

Set Up the All in One SEO Plugin

The All in One SEO plugin is the best tool for optimizing not only the WordPress website home page, but also the inner post pages. It allows you to add a title, description, and keyword Metadata dynamically, without needing to add it manually for each page. You can set up the global options for the All in One SEO from the plugin settings page and you can set up the SEO Metadata for each individual post from each post-editing page. In order to use this plugin, you have to install it from the Plugins section on the WordPress admin page or through FTP.

Set Up the All in One SEO Plugin

Set the Global Metadata

Note: To perform this exercise, you must install the All in One SEO plugin.

1. Position your mouse pointer over **Settings**.

2. Click **All in One SEO** in the pop-up menu.

The Plugin settings appear.

3. Scroll down to the Plugin Status section.

4. Click the **Enabled** option (○ changes to ◉).

5. Type the website title Metadata.

6. Type the website description.

7. Type the website keywords.

8. Scroll down to the usage checklist.

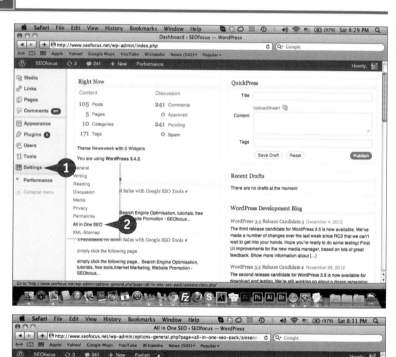

The usage checklist is revealed.

9 Click to deselect the **Use Categories for META keywords** option (☑ changes to ☐).

10 Click the **Use Tags for META keywords** option (☐ changes to ☑).

11 Click the **Dynamically Generate Keywords for Posts Page** option (☐ changes to ☑).

12 Click the **Use noindex for Categories** option (☐ changes to ☑).

13 Click the **Use noindex for Archives** option (☐ changes to ☑).

14 Click the **Use noindex for Tag Archives** option (☐ changes to ☑).

15 Click to deselect the **Autogenerate Descriptions** option (☑ changes to ☐).

16 Click the **Capitalize Category Titles** option (☐ changes to ☑).

17 Scroll down to the end of the page

The end of the setting page appears.

18 Click **Update Options**.

The plugin settings are saved.

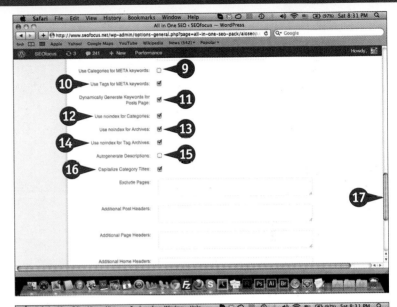

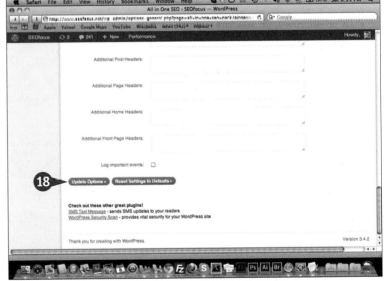

continued ▶ 245

TIP

Which optimized All in One SEO settings should I choose?

The most important All in One SEO plugin global settings are Title, Description, and Keywords, because they appear on the website home page Metadata code. When you type this information, it should include important SEO keywords and follow SEO standards. For example, the title page should be descriptive, yet limited to 70 characters; otherwise, Google will omit the extra characters from the search results. The description should provide general information about the website and should be limited to 155 characters. The last Metadata setting is Keywords, which includes the important keywords in the website. Try to keep the number of keywords as limited as possible; otherwise, it is considered stuffing.

In addition to the All in One options in the plugin setting page, you can apply unique title, description, and keyword Metadata for each post or page that you create for the WordPress website or blog. In the new post page, you can find a section that enables you to set up unique Metadata for this specific post. This unique SEO information increases the page's optimization and its chance of appearing in the search engine results page.

Set Up the All in One SEO Plugin (continued)

Set the Posts Metadata

1 Position your mouse pointer over **Posts**.

2 Click **Add New** in the pop-up menu.

The Add New Post page appears.

3 Type the title of the post.

4 Type the content of the post.

5 Scroll down to the All in One SEO Pack section.

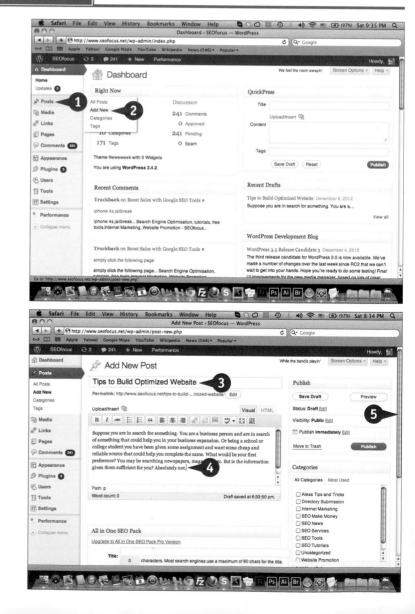

The All in One SEO Pack section appears.

6 Type the title.

7 Type the description.

8 Type the keywords.

9 Scroll up to the top of the page.

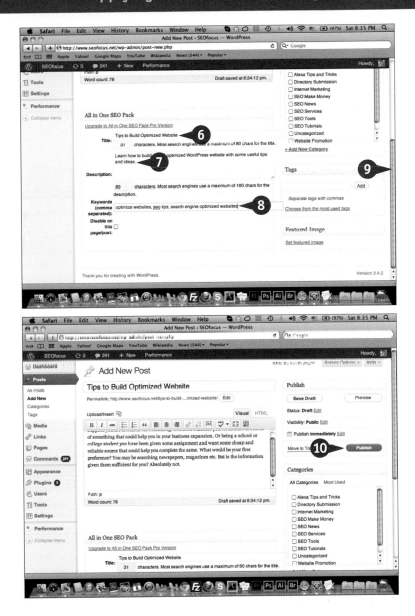

10 At the top of the Add New Post page, click **Publish**.

The new post is published with the specified Metadata applied.

TIP

Can I apply All in One SEO optimization to both pages and posts?
Yes, you can choose to display the All in One SEO Pack section to both posts and pages or either of them. You can set up this in the All in One SEO options from the WordPress settings. While the posts are the main form of content in WordPress, many SEO experts focus on optimizing the posts. The best practice is to optimize all the content on your website.

Set Up Permalinks

The default WordPress URLs are usually numbered and include question mark signs, which means they are search engine optimized less frequently and harder for visitors to recognize. Permalinks help you customize how WordPress generates the URLs for the new posts once you publish them. Instead of using numbers, you can set up WordPress to display the post title, category, or publishing date. You can access the Permalinks from the WordPress General Settings page and customize how you want the post and page URLs to appear.

Set Up Permalinks

1 Click **Settings** on the WordPress admin page.

The WordPress General Settings page appears.

2 Click **Permalinks.**

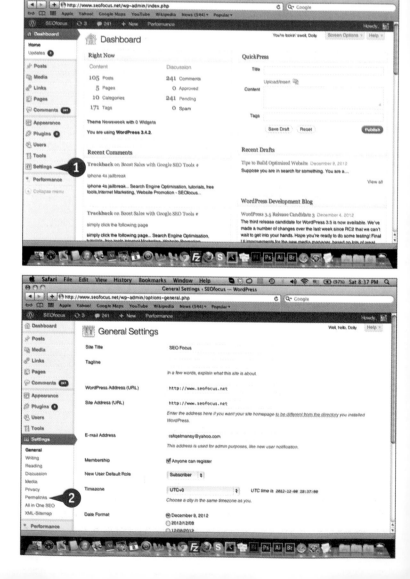

The Permalink Settings page appears.

3 Click the **Post name** option (○ changes to ◉).

4 Click **Save Changes.**

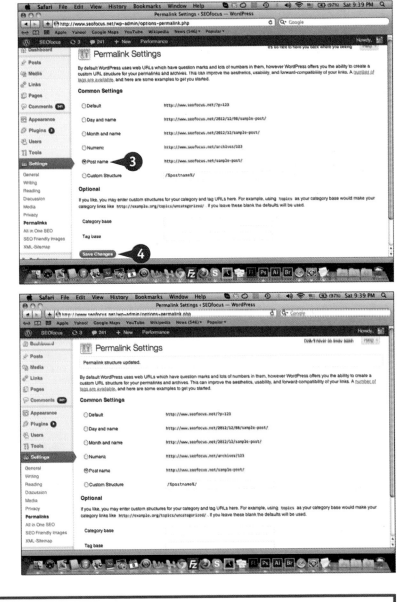

The Permalinks setting is saved.

TIPS

Which is the best Permalinks setting for SEO?
The URLs are important factors in post indexing. They should include the important keywords in your post. So, it is best to set the /%postname%/ post name for permalinks if you want to add it to the custom field. This option sets the URL like the post title, but separated by dashes.

Will the Permalinks updates apply to the old posts?
Yes, when you change the Permalinks from numbers to the post name or other options, old archived posts are updated as well. To confirm this, check the URLs of older posts and see how they have changed.

Install the SEO Friendly Images Plugin

Optimized images can help your website or blog to display in search engines when users type keywords related to your image. You can optimize the images through their image names, size, and Metadata, such as the Alt and Title tags. As with the All in One SEO plugin, you can use the SEO Friendly Images plugin to optimize the images in your WordPress website easily and automatically. You can also use it to automatically add Title and Alt tags for images and set up these tags to be the same as the name of the post or the image.

Install the SEO Friendly Images Plugin

Note: To perform this exercise, you must install the SEO Friendly Images plugin from the Add New page under the Plugins section.

1 Type **www.seofocus.net/ wp-login.php/** in your web browser and press Enter.

2 Type your username.

3 Type your password.

4 Click **Log In.**

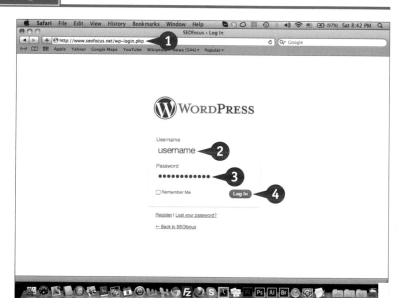

The WordPress Dashboard page appears.

5 Click **Settings.**

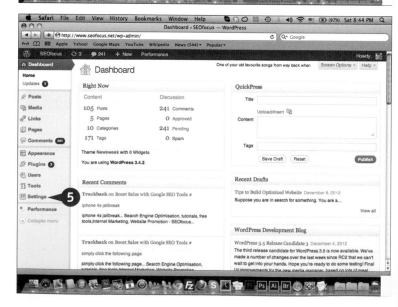

The General Settings page
appears.

6 Click **SEO Friendly Images.**

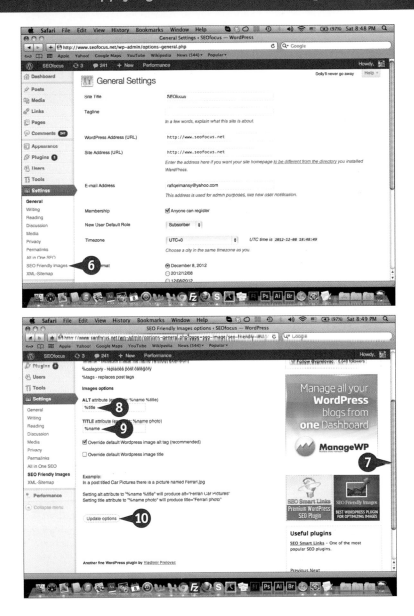

The SEO Friendly Images plugin
settings appear.

7 Scroll down to the Images
options section.

8 Type **%title** in the Alt field.

9 Type **%name** in the Title field.

10 Click **Update options.**

The plugin settings are saved.

TIP

How do I upload an image to a WordPress post or page?
You can upload images to a WordPress post or page in two ways. The first is by clicking the **Upload/Insert**
button on the new post page. The second is through the FTP client in the /wp-content/uploads folder. You
insert the image in the post using the HTML tag `<img src="image path" />` and then add this code
to the post using the HTML viewer.

CHAPTER 13

Monetizing Your Website

The main reason for SEO is to get more traffic and a higher ranking for your website. This traffic turns to potential customers for your product or service. Also, visitors can click advertising banners and promotional links that you can add to your website and get revenues when visitors view or click on it. This concept is known as *monetizing* your website.

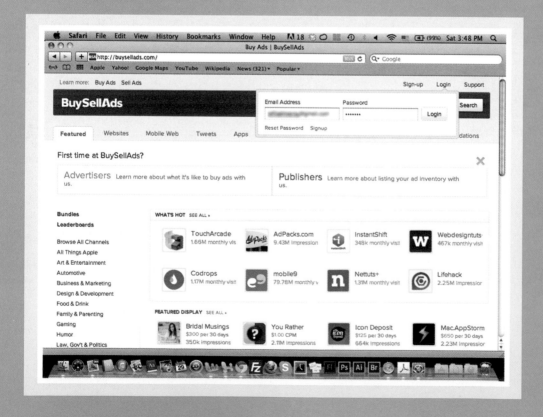

Explore Advertising Revenue Types

While you can direct traffic that comes to your website toward buying a product or service, some websites, particularly magazines and blogs, earn revenue other ways. One is to include advertising spots that promote other sites and services. These spots can be banners, video, text links, or specific articles on your website, such as product reviews. When building your website, you have to consider how to earn revenue from your website or blog and the different types of advertisements that you can place within the website structure. With strategic planning, you can monetize your website, maximizing your profits.

Cost Per Click

In this revenue model, the user clicks an advertising text link or banner, such as an image, text, or video. The advertiser pays the website owner each time users click the mouse and visit the advertiser's product or service website. The *Cost Per Click (CPC)* varies based on many factors, such as the type of visitors coming to the website and website competitors. For example, you can set the cost of a banner click at thirty cents each time a visitor clicks this banner, the advertiser pays you this amount of money. This model does not include how the visitor interacts with the advertiser's product or website; the payment process is complete once the user clicks the banner. Usually, this model is suitable for websites of all sizes that would like to generate revenue from advertising. Visitors with the potential to click banners on your site have the potential to click other links on your site, which can lead to possible revenue. Ad providers such as Google AdSense, Yahoo Publisher Network, and Facebook handle the CPC campaigns for your website.

Cost Per Mille

The *Cost Per Mille (CPM)*, or the cost per thousand, impressions model refers to the cost that an advertiser pays a website owner to display the advertiser's banner on the website owner's site to visitors a thousand times. For example, an advertiser pays you to display his banner for a number of website users regardless of whether they click the banner or not; these displays are known as *banner impressions*. These impressions do not include actions such as refreshing the page from the user's browser. Therefore, if you sell 1,000 impressions on your website for $2 and the advertiser buys 10,000 impressions, he will pay a total of $20 to you for displaying the banner to 10,000 of your website visitors. CPM is most profitable if your website receives a lot of traffic or page views because you can sell large numbers of impressions to different advertisers, and use rotating ads methods to display multiple ads in the same advertising area. CPM ad providers include Facebook and BuySellAds that deliver advertising banners to your website.

Cost Per Action

The *Cost Per Action (CPA)* is commonly used by advertising networks and it refers to an advertising campaign that pays you when your website visitors click the advertiser's banner, which links them to the advertiser's site, and then conducts a specific process. This process can be buying a product from the advertiser's store, which is known as *Cost Per Sale (CPS)*, or it can be completing a form to sign up for a service or information or completing a survey page, which is known as *Cost Per Lead (CPL)*. Most affiliate marketing campaigns are based on this model: they only pay the website owner once visitors respond to the ad by buying a product or completing a form or survey. If your website is new and does not have much potential traffic, you will not be able to generate good revenue from this type of ad. You first must build trust with website visitors in order for them to click links on your website and trust the products being advertised.

Effective Cost Per Mille

While the Cost Per Mille (CPM) equals the display of a banner a thousand times to clients, the *Effective Cost Per Mille (eCPM)* refers to the action a user takes after clicking the banner. The eCPM is calculated by dividing the total earnings by the total number of impressions in thousands. For example, if an advertiser earns $3 from users' actions, and the ad appears 1,000 times, the formula for calculating the eCPM is $3/1,000 *1,000 where 1,000 is constant, and the results of the Cost-Per-Click in this model is $3.

Fixed-Price Banners

The fixed-price banner model means the advertiser pays a fixed amount for placing their banners on your website for a period of time that is usually one month or more. In this case, the cost is paid in advance regardless of the number of clicks or impressions the banner receives. The more clicks the banner receives, the greater the possibility that the advertisers renew their banner placements for additional months. The advertisers choose which websites to place their ads on based on a number of factors, such as the amount of traffic the website receives, the category of the website, and the impressions that each page receives. The fixed-price model is one of the easiest advertising models because you do not need to join an advertising network to implement it; all you need to do is contact advertisers and invite them to advertise on your website. There are some networks, such as BuySellAds, that help you market your website banner zones and provide easy management platform for your banners.

Consider the Advertising Formats

You can choose from a variety of web advertisement formats when choosing the ads that will appear on your website. Each ad format can have a different impact on the website visitors. You may notice that users click a specific ad format more than the others. Subsequently, you can test each format and decide which is best for your website based on the number of user clicks and overall traffic responding to the ad format. Generally, the ad format is an image, text, video, or specific HTML page that appears before displaying the targeted website or a new web page for the advertiser.

Text Ads

Text ads are text-based hyperlinks on your website that advertisers buy, and when visitors click them, they go to the advertiser's website. Text ads do not include graphical images but sometimes include text descriptions that appear under the main link. Text ads are sold directly to the advertiser by the website owner or through ad networks such as AdSense.

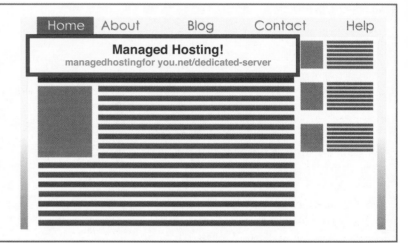

Image Ads

Image ads, or display ads, are ad banners that use graphic images instead of text links. Image ads are available in several standard sizes. While you can create banners without restricting them to standard sizes, it is recommended you follow the standard dimensions so you create banner areas that are suitable for different customers. Image ads attract the visitor's eyes to a banner, often leading them to click it.

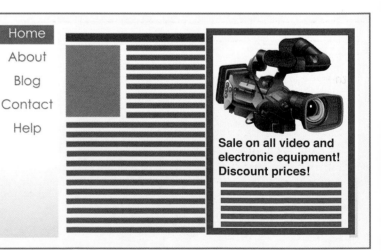

Flash Ads

Flash ads refer to banners that use Flash technology to create animated ads and motion graphics. Flash ads are more attractive than the ordinary still images or text ads. However, they do not appear in smartphone and tablet devices that do not support Flash, which makes this format undesirable for clients targeting smartphone and tablet users. Alternatively, some clients use HTML5 animated ads as a substitution for Flash ads because it viewable on smartphones and devices that do not support Flash.

Video Ads

As the Internet speeds increase, making it easier to use rich media such as video, many advertisers create video ads to attract users and deliver direct, interactive messages. However, it is not recommended you use a video ad more than once on a website page; otherwise it may cause the page to load slowly and distract the website visitor.

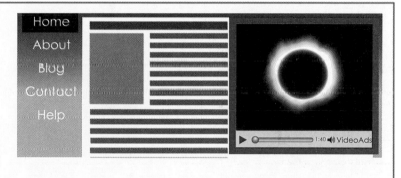

E-mail Ads

With the increase in the value of e-mail marketing, many advertisers are considering sponsoring e-mail newsletters as a marketing method for their products. This is done by sending e-mail newsletters that advise users to use a specific product or service. Also, the e-mail ads can list advertiser services or products with a link to purchase it. A popular directory is the Yahoo Directory at http://dir.yahoo.com.

Create AdSense Ads

*G*oogle *AdSense* is the most commonly used ad provider. You can use it to earn revenue from your website blog by placing AdSense text and image ads. These ads are delivered through the Google Display Network, where advertisers create ads using Google AdWords, and display them on your website. AdSense allows you to create ad zones, filter ads, and handle payments. Google AdSense displays ads on your website based on a number of factors, such as the category of the website and the keywords that appear in the web page content. You can also use AdSense to deliver advertisements to mobile sites.

Create AdSense Ads

1 Type **www.google.com/ adsense** in your web browser and press `Enter`.

2 Type your e-mail address.

3 Type your password.

4 Click **Sign in.**

Note: If you do not have an account, click **Sign Up Now.** It can take up to a week for the account to be approved.

The AdSense home page appears.

5 Click **My ads.**

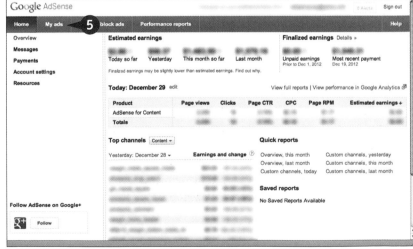

The My ads page appears.

6 Click **New ad unit.**

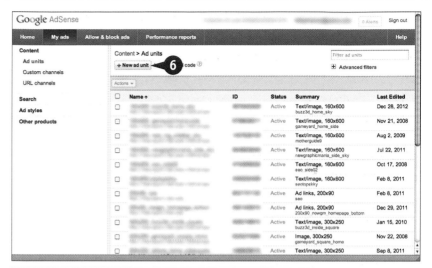

The Create new ad unit page appears.

7 Type the name of the AdSense unit.

8 Click the **Ad size** pop-up menu and select the size of the AdSense unit.

9 Click the **Backup ads** pop-up menu and select Show blank space.

10 Click the **Create new custom channel** link.

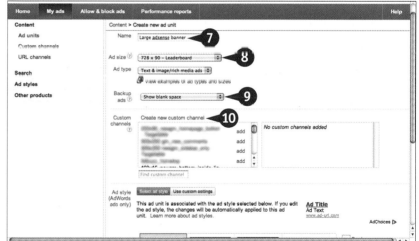

continued ▶

Create AdSense Ads (continued)

Google AdSense provides two main advertisement choices and you can display either or both on your website or blog. One is text ads, which appear as text links in the AdSense advertising spots and include promotional descriptions about a product. With text ads, you can display more than one ad in the same advertising spot. The other is image ads, which are image banners with still and animated images. While the image ads are more attractive, each AdSense spot includes only one ad. This can narrow your chances of getting clicks on the ad banner.

Create AdSense Ads (continued)

The Add new custom channel dialog box appears.

⑪ Type the name of the channel.

⑫ Click **Save.**

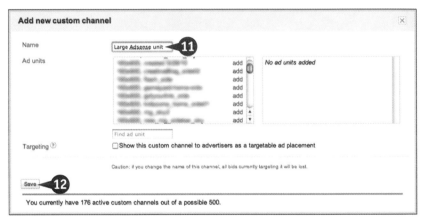

The Create new ad unit page reappears.

⑬ Scroll down.

The Ad style section comes into view.

14 Click an ad style.

15 Click **Save and get code.**

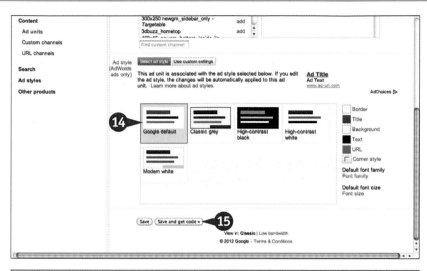

The code appears. You can copy the code and paste it in your website where you want the AdSense ad to appear.

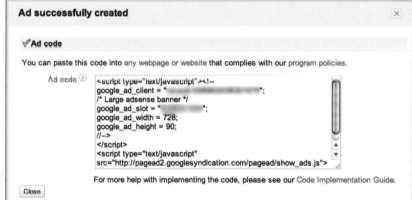

How can I determine if text ads or image ads are better?

Choosing to display text ads, image ads, or both depends on how each type of ad performs on your website. The standard choice is to allow both image and text ads in the AdSense zone. But in some cases, you may notice that website visitors click specific types of ads more than others. Subsequently, you get more revenue from one particular type. The best practice is to test all the types of AdSense ads on your website and choose the one that best suits your website content and audience.

Modify Existing AdSense Ads

One of the advantages of using AdSense that it lets you easily handle and manage the ads from their platform without having to edit the ad code manually. When you create an AdSense ad, you can easily modify it, even after you add it to your website or page. When you click the My ads page, you can filter different AdSense ads or search for specific ads by name, edit them, and set them up to display either text, images, or both. Also, you can get the ad code by clicking Get Code.

Modify Existing AdSense Ads

1 Click **My ads** on the AdSense home page.

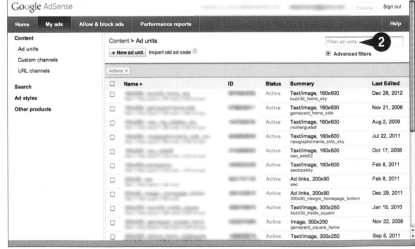

The My Ads page appears

2 Type the name of the ad in the Filter ad units field.

The specified ad appears.

3 Click the ad name.

The ad settings page appears where you can modify your ad options.

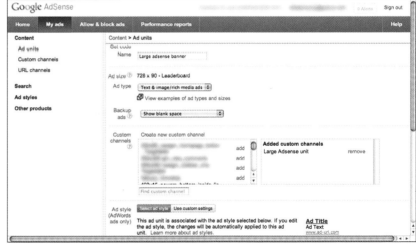

Block AdSense Advertisers' URLs

You may need to block inappropriate ads from your website. Google AdSense enables you to block up to 500 domain names. When you block a main domain, all its pages and subdomains are also blocked. You can learn about blocking URLs at https://support.google.com/adsense/bin/answer. py?hl=en&utm_medium=link&utm_campaign=ww-ww-et-asfe_&utm_source=aso&answer=164657. It is very important not to click the AdSense ads on your website. This can cause the suspending of your entire AdSense account. Instead, you can preview the ads using the Google Publisher toolbar at https://support.google.com/adsense/bin/answer.py?hl=en&answer=2415249&topic=2414281&ctx=topic.

Block AdSense Advertisers' URLs

1 Type **www.google.com/ adsense** in your web browser and press Enter.

2 Type your e-mail address.

3 Type your password.

4 Click **Sign in.**

The AdSense home page appears.

5 Click **Allow & block ads.**

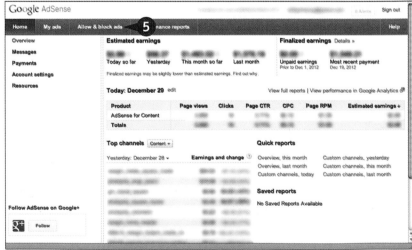

The Advertiser URLs tab appears.

6 Type the URL of the ad you would like to block.

7 Click **Block URLs.**

Note: You can add multiple URLs, each on a separate line.

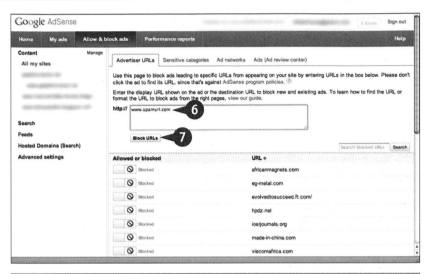

A The ad appears in the blocked URLs list.

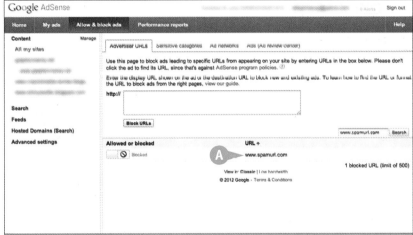

How many AdSense ads are permitted on a web page?
AdSense limits the number of the ads that you can display on your web page to three ads and three ad lines that appear as vertical or horizontal text links. If you are running your ads through third-party ad networks or have different combinations in your ad display, you can go over this limit.

How can I disable and then enable an ad?
Sometimes you would like to disable a specific ad display for a period of time and then allow it again later. In this case, you can disable the website URL from the Advertisers URLs. Then, you can toggle the **Block** button next to the blocked URL to allow it again.

Block Ads Using the Ad Review Center

Given Google can ban your account if you click your own website, it makes it difficult to review different ads on your website or blog. The *Ad review center* in AdSense enables you to review the ads that appear in your website, as well as block and unblock ads. You can also filter the ad view to display image ads, text ads, or rich media ads that refer to animated Flash banners. You can also filter the ads based on their similarities with specific ads or banner images or based on their display dates.

Block Ads Using the Ad Review Center

1 Type **www.google.com/ adsense** in your web browser and press **Enter**.

2 Type your e-mail address.

3 Type your password.

4 Click **Sign in.**

The AdSense home page appears.

5 Click the **Allow & block ads** tab.

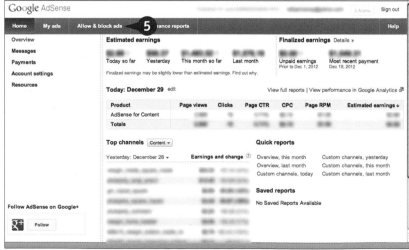

The Advertiser URLs tab appears.

6 Click the **Ads (Ad review center)** tab.

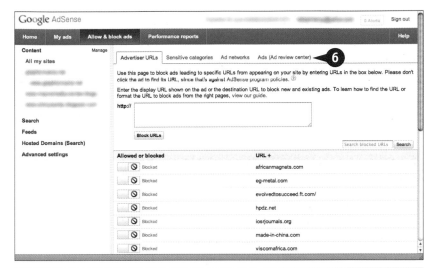

The Ad review center tab appears.

7 Position your mouse pointer over an ad and click **Block** when it appears.

The ad is blocked and hidden from your website.

What are Made For AdSense ads?

Made For AdSense (MFA) ads are inexpensive ads that appear on your website for a very low Cost-Per-Click. These ads can reduce your revenue, especially when you have too many ads on your website. You can use the AdSense filter tools to remove ads that are unrelated to your website niche.

How do I filter ads in the Ad review center?

You can filter the ads that appear in the Ad review center to review them easily. Click the **Filters** link on the right side of the Ad review center. Select different filter options and then click **Apply filters** to display the ads.

Position AdSense Ads

Ad placement varies from website to website, but specific positions on websites can drive more clicks than others. Therefore, you should understand your website's structure and which AdSense ad placement positions visitors will notice and then click. Research indicates you should place important elements above the web *page fold*, the portion of the website users see first, without needing to scroll down the page. Putting AdSense ads above the fold can result in more user clicks. The mobile devices have different screen sizes. Thus, you have to consider this in testing your adsense placement.

Position AdSense Ads

① Type **http://as-abovethefold. appspot.com** in your web browser and press **Enter**.

The Above the Fold page appears.

② Type the website name in the field.

③ Click **Go**.

The website preview appears.

4 Scroll down the page.

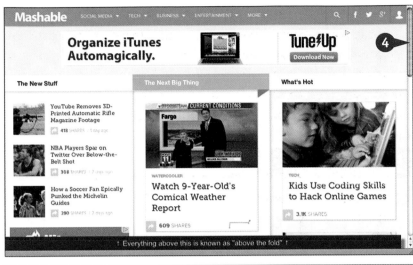

A The hidden sections of the website appear below the fold.

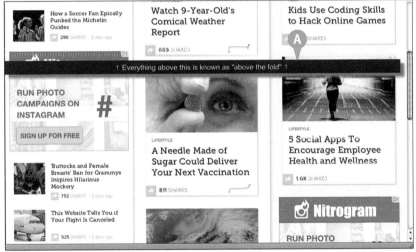

What is the AdSense heat map?

The *heat map* is a Google map showing positions on your website structure that can benefit from AdSense. You can find the map at http://support.google.com/adsense/bin/answer.py?hl=en&answer=1354747. The best areas to put AdSense on your website or blog appear above the folds.

How do I check the different AdSense standard sizes?

You can review some standard sizes before creating an AdSense unit. Based on these standard sizes and the ad placement guidelines, you can determine which ad size to use and where to put it on your website. You can preview different Google AdSense standard sizes at http://support.google.com/adsense/bin/answer.py?hl=en&answer=185665&topic=29561&ctx=topic.

Create Chitika Ads

The ad network Chitika provides text and image advertisements based on Click-Per-Cost, similar to Google AdSense. You sign up on Chitika as a publisher (https://chitika.com/publishers), and create ads to match your website structure. Chitika works best for websites receiving most of their traffic from the United States. You can set up Chitika to display alternative ads when no ads are served from their network. The Chitika dashboard gives you detailed information about each ad's performance, and you can create a channel for each ad to better track it.

Create Chitika Ads

1. Type **http://chitika.com** in your web browser and press `Enter`.

The Chitika website appears.

2. Click **My Account.**

The Login page appears.

3 Type your username.

4 Type your password.

5 Click **Login**.

Note: You can click **Apply Now** from the Publishers tab to create a new account.

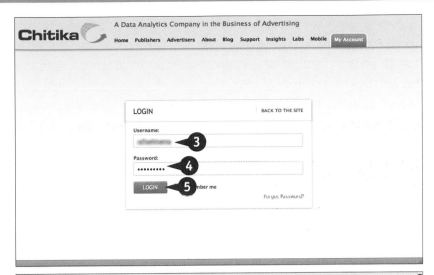

The account dashboard appears.

6 Position your mouse pointer over **Ad Setup**.

7 Click **Types of Ads**.

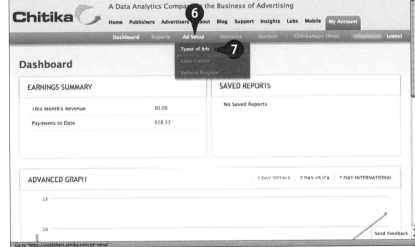

TIP

What are the different ad levels in Chitika?
Chitika publishers have three ad levels. The Silver is the default approved level. The Bronze is the lower level. The Gold is the highest level on which you can maximize your ad revenues. The Gold level is where you want to move your website. You can submit your website for review for Golden-Level qualification by clicking **Domains** in the My Account menu or visiting https://publishers.chitika.com/domains. You can add domains to review by using the form there. It is important to review the Chitika information when establishing your account settings and payment method and to use the code in your website or blog.

continued ▶

Create Chitika Ads (continued)

T̲he Chitika ad set-up page includes different options for customizing your ad zone. In the first part, you customize the ad's colors, such as the link color, text color, background color, and border color. In the second part, you choose the ad size from more than 20 size options, the type of ad, and the *fallback*, which refers to the content Chitika uses to fill the banner when no banner is served. You can fill the ad area with Chitika fallback links or alternative URL links. The third part is the reporting section, where you set up channel information.

Create Chitika Ads (continued)

The Ad Setup/Our Ad Types page appears.

8 Click **Get Started.**

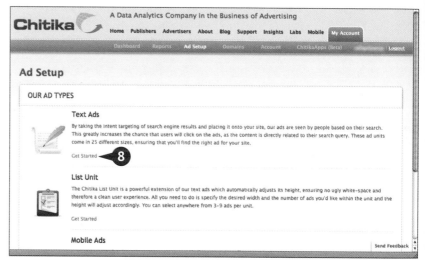

The Ad Setup/Code Generator page appears.

9 Set up the ad properties by picking your colors, selecting unit options, and adding a reporting category.

10 Scroll down the page.

⑪ Click **Get Code.**

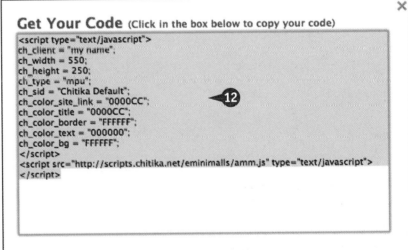

The Get Your Code dialog box appears.

⑫ Click and drag to select the code and then press ⌘+C (Ctrl+C) to copy.

You can paste the ad code in your website HTML page to display the Chitika ad.

Are there any other ad networks?
AdBrite is a marketplace for publishers and advertisers to exchange ads. You can visit AdBrite at www. adbrite.com and sign up as a publisher to add banners on your website. Then you can submit your website ad zones, control ad prices, and approve or reject ads. You add the ads by pasting HTML code. Ad buyers can buy banner space by clicking your ad links directly or through the AdBrite marketplace. Similar to Chitika and AdSense, you can modify ad zone styles and sizes to match your website's structure and color themes. AdBrite provides different types of ads, such as full-page ads, CPM banners, CPC banners (text or images), and video banners.

Work with Commission Conjunction

*C*ommission Conjunction is a Click-Per-Action and Pay-Per-Call network that pays you when your website visitors click a banner or link and make a purchase. After you create a publisher account, you can join any of the advertisers' campaigns to get revenues through their banners and use their different ad formats, which vary from image banners to promotional links. Each link or promotion gets a unique URL that you can track from the Commission Conjunction dashboard to check your revenue. This network works well for websites with a lot of targeted traffic.

Work with Commission Conjunction

1 Type **www.cj.com** in your web browser and press <kbd>Enter</kbd>.

2 Click **Login.**

3 Type your username.

4 Type your password.

5 Click **Login.**

Note: If you do not have a publisher account, you can create an account at www.cj.com/publisher-signup-form.

The Commission Junction home page appears.

6 Click the **Get Links** tab.

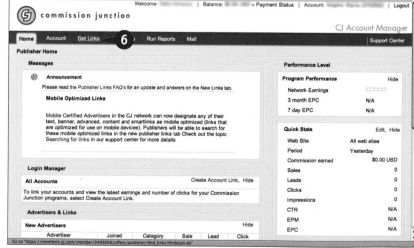

The General Categories tab appears.

7 Type **Microsoft** in the Search Advertiser field.

8 Click **Find.**

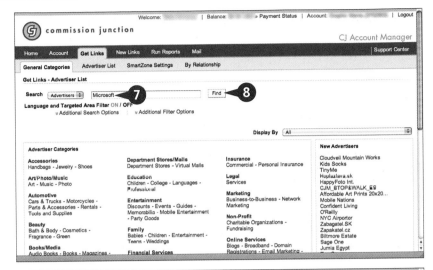

The Advertiser Search Results appear.

9 Click the **Apply to Program** option next to any advertising campaign (☐ changes to ☑).

10 Click **Apply to Program.**

After you are approved to the advertiser program, you can choose one or more of the advertisers ads code to add in your website.

TIP

What is Clickbank and how can I get traffic from it?

Clickbank (www.clickbank.com) is a CPA marketplace where you can find advertisers that provide revenue based on each purchase of their product. Simply get the customized advertisers link and add it in your website as a text link or within an image banner. When visitors click it, you are paid a specific percentage of the sales. For example, if one of your website visitors clicks an advertiser's link, visits the product website, and completes a purchase, you get 25 percent of the product price. Clickbank is one of the most famous and most profitable marketplaces you can use, especially when you promote products related to yours to your visitors.

Work with BuySellAds

BuySellAds is an advertising network that includes a comprehensive marketplace for active advertisers and publishers in various categories. You can apply as a publisher based on the amount of traffic and impressions your website receives. BuySellAds delivers both Cost Per Mille (CPM) and fixed-price ads. You can sign up and submit your website, which is known as *Property*. Then, you can create multiple ad zones for each website, which are known as *Inventory*. Once you create an ad zone, you receive two snippets of codes to install on your website per the placement guidelines.

Work with BuySellAds

Submit a Website to BuySellAds

1 Type **http://buysellads.com** in your web browser and press **Enter**.

2 Click **Login.**

3 Type your e-mail address.

4 Type your password.

5 Click **Login.**

Note: If you do not have an account, click **Sign-up** to create an account.

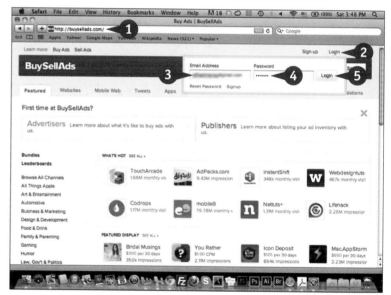

The BuySellAds page appears.

6 Position your mouse pointer over your account name.

7 Click **Dashboard.**

The Dashboard page appears.

8 Click **Dashboard.**

9 Click **Add Property.**

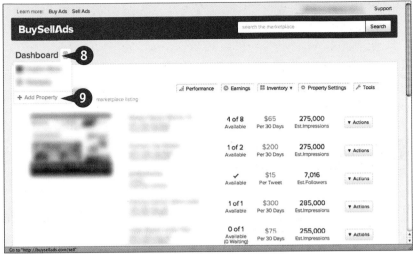

The Add Property form appears.

10 Type the requested website information into the form, scrolling down as you go.

11 Click **Submit.**

After your website is approved, you will see it listed in the Publisher Dashboard.

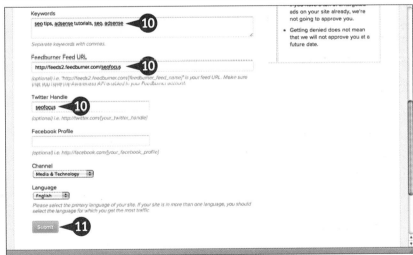

TIP

What are the available ad zone sizes?
BuySellAds provides a wide range of ad sizes that vary from small 125×125 pixel banners to a large 160× 600 pixel skyscrapers. You can also set a custom ad zone size, but it is recommended you use the standard sizes to have a better chance of selling banners on your website. When you offer standard sizes, advertisers can use their own standard banners without needing to make size modifications.

continued ▶

BuySellAds provides a wide range of types of ads, such as website ads, mobile-based ads, iOS and android app ads, RSS feed ads, desktop ads, e-mail ads, and Twitter-sponsored tweets. Each type has specific settings. Once you create an ad, you can set up ad requests from advertisers to be approved automatically or manually. Once an advertiser submits a placement request, you receive a notice. After you approve the ad, it appears in the ad zone on your website. In the automatic approval, you do not have to approve the ad manually, as it appears once the advertiser buys the ad zone.

Work with BuySellAds (continued)

Create an Advertising Zone

1 On the Dashboard page, position your mouse pointer over **Inventory.**

2 Click **Add Inventory.**

A new advertising zone form appears.

3 Click the pop-up menus, select options, and then type the requested information to fill in the form.

4 Scroll down the page.

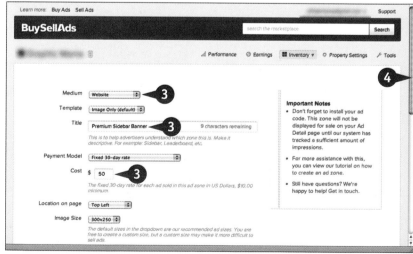

5 Continue typing in the requested information and selecting options from the pop-up menus to complete the form.

6 Click **Next.**

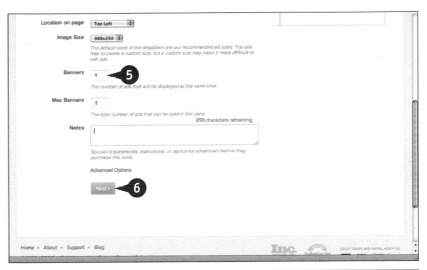

In the Style Settings section, the ad zone code appears.

7 Click **Save.**

The ad zone is created. You can see the code that you will need to paste into your website HTML page.

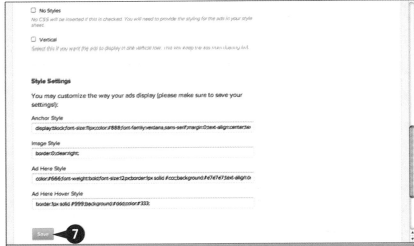

TIPS

How do I install the BuySellAds code?
The BuySellAds ad zone code consists of two parts. The first code snippet applies to all your website banners and is added to your website HTML code just after the opening `<body>` tag. You can add the second code snippet in the place where you would like the ad zone to display.

How do I change the banner display options?
You can change the number of ad banners that appear in one zone by adjusting the setting in the ad inventory setting form. You can set the ad zone style by clicking the **Action** pop-up menu next to each ad zone in the inventory and then clicking the **Ad Code** link.

CHAPTER 14

Building and Managing an SEO Team

If you have a large website, it is important to consider either hiring a team to work with you or hiring a SEO company to help you optimize your website.

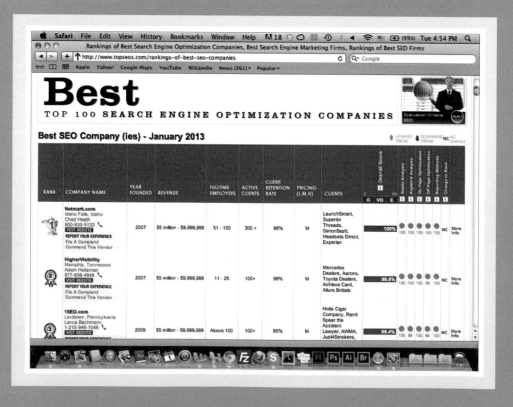

Find the Best SEO Companies

When you search for an SEO company to help you optimize your website, you need to make sure it is trustworthy and professional. You do not want to hire a company that might perform the wrong SEO steps or take your money for doing virtually nothing. Thus, finding the right SEO company for your needs means reviewing different companies in the market. You can do this by reading reviews of SEO companies or visiting trusted SEO forums that recommend SEO companies to hire. The /www.topseos.com website lists the best web marketing service providers based on categories, including the SEO companies.

Find the SEO Best Companies

1 Type **www.topseos.com** in the web browser and press **Enter**.

The TopSEOs page appears.

2 Position your mouse pointer over **View Rankings.**

3 Click **Search Engine Optimization.**

The Top 100 SEO Companies page appears.

④ Click one of the companies.

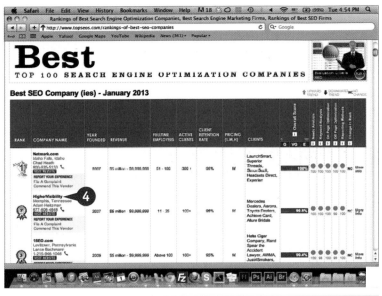

The SEO company information and reviews appears.

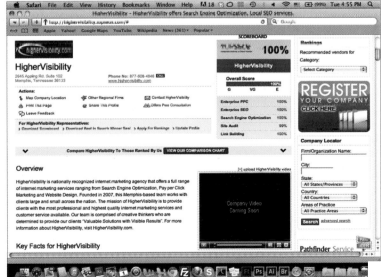

How can I determine the best SEO based on cost?

While many SEO companies are very expensive due to their reputation and clients, you can still find good SEO companies that are more affordable. To lower your costs, you must know what your website needs and then ask for the specific SEO options only; for example, you can request quotes for link building.

Where can I find other good SEO companies?

You can find suggestions for the best SEO companies to use on SEO forums that cover optimization topics; for example, https://forums.digitalpoint.com and www.webmasterworld.com. If you are a paid subscriber of the Warrior Forum (www.warriorforum.com), you can receive professional SEO advice.

Hire an SEO Expert on Elance

If you do not want to hire an entire company and spend a lot of money on SEO techniques that you can do yourself, you can simply hire an SEO expert to assist you in optimizing your website. You can use someone who works remotely, which means the person works from a different location outside your company and delivers the work through the Internet, and as an independent contractor. One of the services you can use to hire an independent contractor is Elance at www.elance.com. On the website, you can hire a SEO expert or post a job request, and other experts can apply for your job.

Hire an SEO Expert on Elance

1 Type **https://www.elance.com** in the web browser and press **Enter**.

The Elance page appears.

2 Click **Sign In.**

Note: If you do not already have an account, you can create one by clicking the **Join** link in the top-right of the Elance web page.

The Welcome to Elance Sign In page appears.

3 Type your username or E-mail address.

4 Type your password.

5 Click **Sign In.**

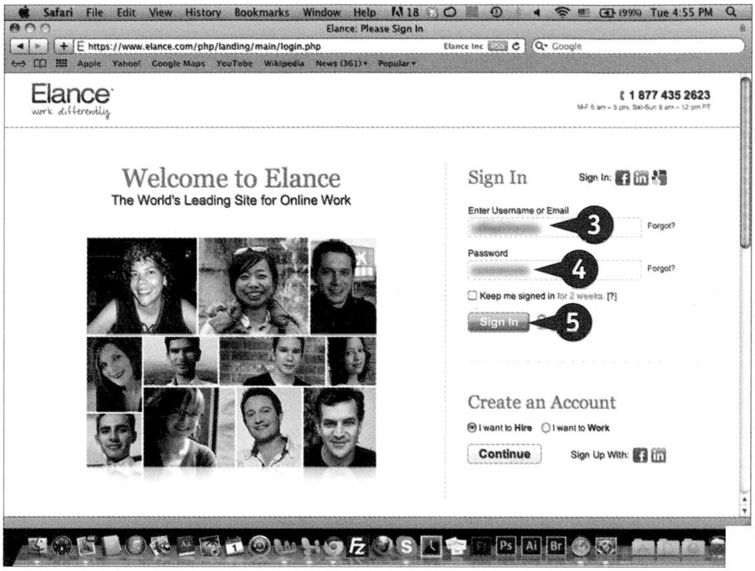

Your Elance personal page appears.

6 Position your mouse pointer over **Hire.**

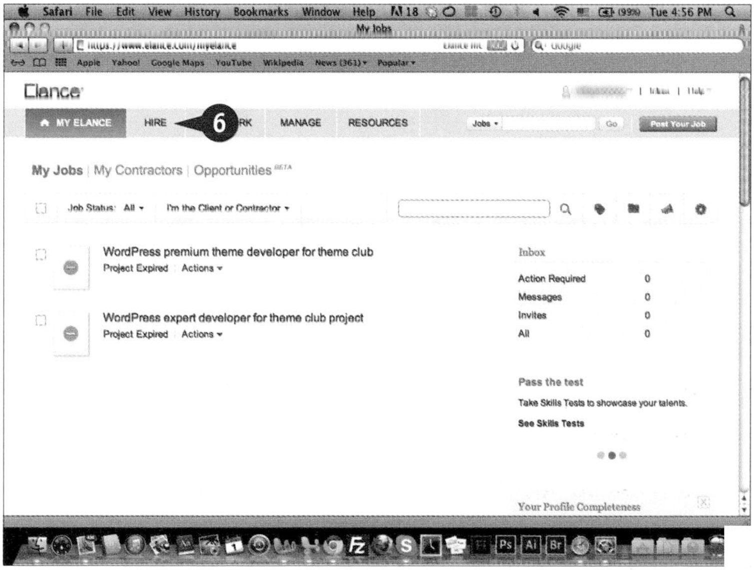

TIP

What are Elance contractors?

When you sign up in Elance for the first time, you will have to choose whether you want to create an account to find a job or hire others for your own projects. The experts that you hire for the job are called *contractors*, and can be either individuals or companies. Contractor profiles will help you determine if the contractor is a person or a company. Some people prefer to hire an individual person, because they can follow the work more closely and contact one person directly, whereas often with a company, a technical person is not provided as a contact.

continued ▶

Hire an SEO Expert on Elance (continued)

Elance provides a marketplace, with many categories, where professionals and employers can meet. When you try to find a good SEO service provider, you must search for prospects with strong skills and experience with projects and websites similar to yours. Some SEO experts are only good at promoting small sites, while others can really help with websites that are larger and more complex. To find an SEO expert who matches your needs, either search for candidates using the left menu options or type **SEO** in the search field at the top of the search contractor page.

Hire an SEO Expert on Elance (continued)

7 Click **Search Contractors**.

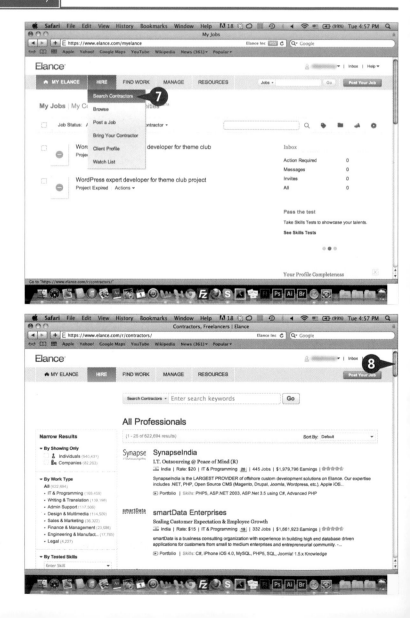

The Search Contractors page appears.

8 Scroll down to the By Tested Skills menu on the left.

The By Tested Skills menu comes into view.

⑨ Click the down arrow (▾) and select Search Engine Optimization from the drop-down list.

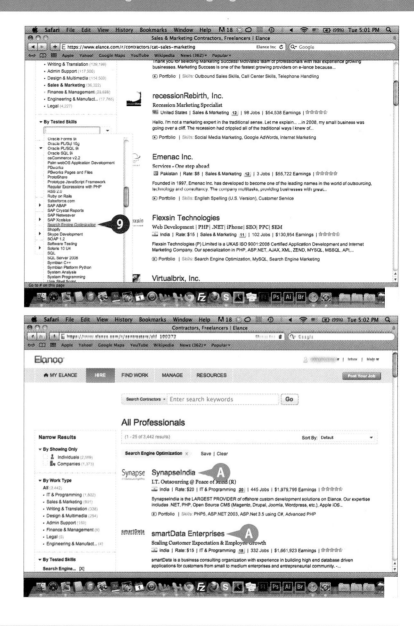

Ⓐ The SEO contractors appear.

How do I explore experts by category or skills?

You can explore the individuals and companies listed on Elance based on categories or professional skills. You can do this using the left menu on the Contractors search page, or you can click the **Hire** menu link and then click **Browse** in the submenu. On the Browse page, you can search contractors by business category. You can also narrow your search by clicking the **Skills** link, which lets you search the database of available skills. You review all the skills listed on a page and click the one you need.

Post a Job on Elance

Along with searching for experts on Elance, you can also add a job posting where you include details about your project and outline the SEO help that you need for your website. When contractors see your job post, they apply to it with their cost bids and you are notified. Then you can review and communicate with each contractor to choose the best fit for the job and the price that works with your budget. After you reach an agreement with one of the contractors, you are ready to assign him the job.

Post a Job on Elance

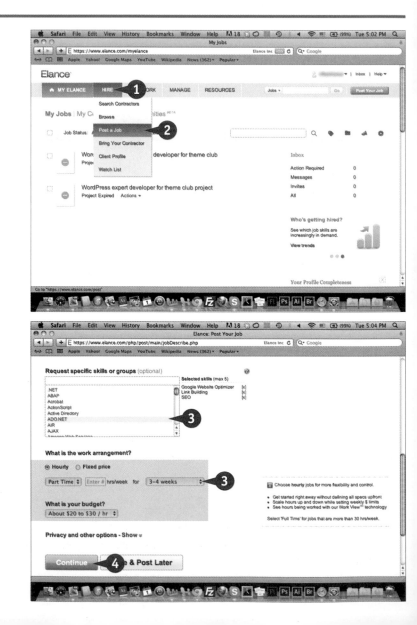

1 Position your mouse pointer over **Hire**.

2 Click **Post a Job**.

The Job Description form appears.

3 Complete the form by clicking and selecting your options.

4 Click **Continue**.

The Job Verify package selection appears.

⑤ Click **Select** to choose the package of your choice.

Note: When you choose the Verified package, a Verification Seal appears next to your profile to help you attract more candidates, as well as indicate that you are serious about the job.

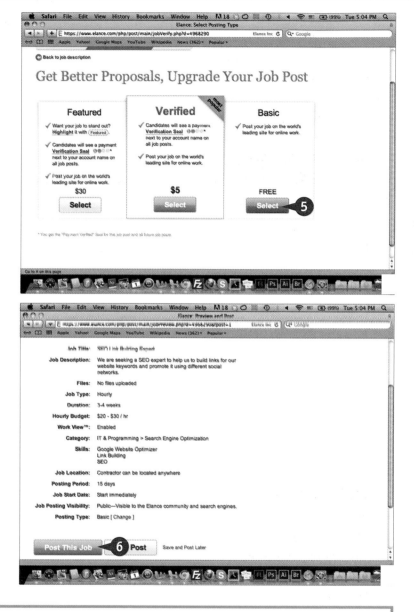

The Job Preview page appears.

⑥ Click **Post This Job.**

After the job is approved by the Elance team, you will start receiving bids from contractors and freelancers who are interested.

TIP

What is the difference between an hourly and a fixed rate?
There are two payment models in Elance as well as most other freelance websites. The first payment model is the *hourly rate*, which refers to paying the contractor based on the number of hours that she works. With this method, you have to monitor the contractor to make sure that the hours she works match the amount of work completed and the money spent. The second payment model is the *fixed cost*, where you pay a set amount of money for a specific job. With this method, you do not pay for each hour. Instead, you pay for the whole project at once.

Hire an SEO Expert on oDesk

Odesk is another online workplace website that connects you with different experts and service buyers around the world, including ones in SEO and web marketing services. oDesk allows you to search for contractors among their huge database or you can post a job contractors can apply for. It has a wide database of users because it is free and it does not require payments from contractors. Instead it takes a 10 percent charge from the contractor's rate or the job revenue if it is a fixed rate job. When you search online for SEO help, it is wise to consider various online workspace websites; this way you can find the best, and most reliable, contractors.

Hire an SEO Expert on oDesk

1 Type **https://www.odesk.com** in the web browser and press **Enter**.

2 Click **Log in.**

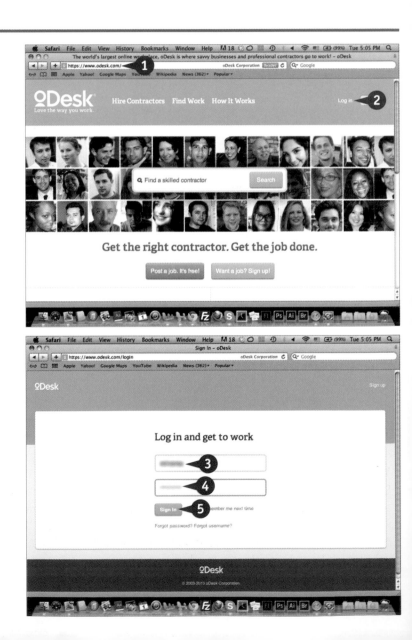

The oDesk login page appears.

3 Type your username.

4 Type your password.

5 Click **Sign In.**

Note: If you do not have an account, click **Sign up** to create an account. Make sure to click **I need a contractor** to create a buyer profile, post jobs, and search contractors.

The oDesk home page appears.

6 Click **Find Contractors.**

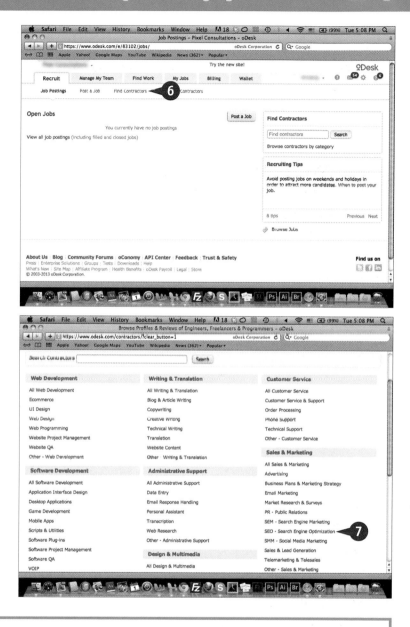

The categories appear.

7 Click **SEO - Search Engine Optimization.**

The contractors with SEO skills database link appears.

What is the oDesk Team application?

Buyers can use the oDesk Team application to track how far along a contractor is on the job. The tool records the contractor's progress using screenshots of the contractor's screen that are taken every few minutes. Then, you can preview these information through the Work Diary next to your current jobs' list. Also, once the employer reviews and approves a contractor's hours for the week, payments can be issued automatically. This tool helps give both employers and contractors confidence that the project is on track, enabling them to focus on the work process instead of payment and time-related issues.

Post an SEO Job on oDesk

When you post a job listing on oDesk, include the SEO help you seek, job details, the skills you need, and the estimated cost and timeframe. You can post the job for all public contractors to view or set it to remain hidden. With a hidden job, you invite contractors to review the job; therefore, public contractors cannot see it or apply for it. When you identify potential contractors, you can interview them through different channels, including e-mail; phone interviews; Skype, Yahoo, and MSN chat applications; and conference applications such as Adobe Connect and WebEx.

Post an SEO Job on oDesk

① On the oDesk buyer profile home page, click **Post a Job**.

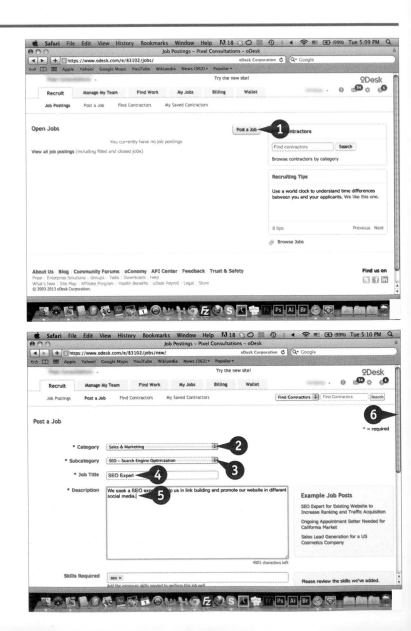

The new job form appears.

② Click the **Category** pop-up menu and select Sales & Marketing.

③ Click the **Subcategory** pop-up menu and select SEO - Search Engine Optimization.

④ Type the job title.

⑤ Type the job description.

⑥ Scroll down to complete the form.

7 Type the desired skills.

8 Click the **Job Type** option to select the job type (○ changes to ◉).

9 Click the **Estimated Duration** pop-up menu and select the duration of the job.

10 Click the **Estimated Workload** pop-up menu and select the number of hours per week.

11 Click the **Contractor Preference** options that apply to the position (☐ changes to ☑).

12 Click the **Job Post Visibility** option to determine who can view the job posting (○ changes to ◉).

13 Click **Post a Job.**

The Job appears in your profile. After oDesk approves it, you will start to receive contractor submissions for the job.

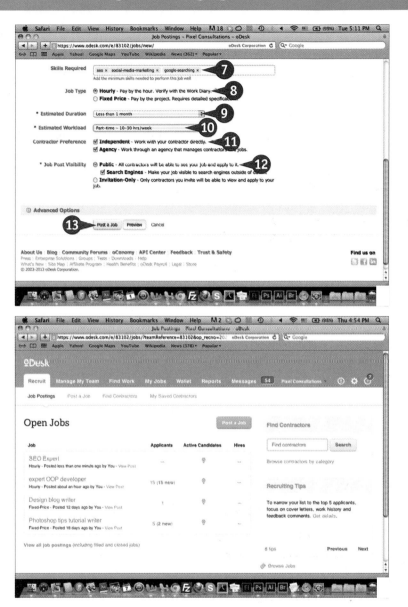

TIP

What is the workload rate?

The *workload rate* refers to the number of hours that the contractor needs to work during the week. Many contractors have other job obligations. You need to include the estimated workload in order to give the contractor a clear vision of your project. The workload varies from task to task, especially in the SEO process. Most SEO tasks require the contractor to check your website over several days to follow up with the changes, so you have to account for this as well.

Create a Freedcamp Project

The SEO process is complex and requires you to do a lot of small tasks on a regular basis until you achieve your target results. Therefore, it is important to manage the workflow for these tasks well, especially when there is a team helping you. Many project management tools help you keep up-to-date with your team's progress. One of these free, comprehensive tools is Freedcamp, which allows you to create multiple projects and add tasks to each one. It also allows you to invite team members to work on projects and manage them through the Freedcamp platform.

Create a Freedcamp Project

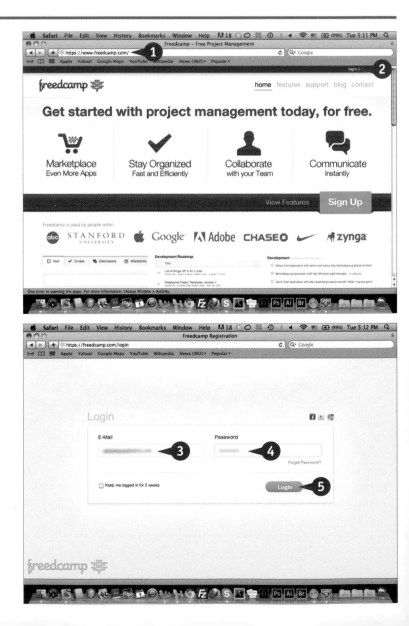

1 Type **www.freedcamp.com** in your web browser and press `Enter`.

2 Click **Login**.

Note: If you do not have an account, click **Sign Up** to create a new account.

The Login page appears.

3 Type your e-mail address.

4 Type your password.

5 Click **Login.**

The Dashboard page appears.

6 Click **Create Project.**

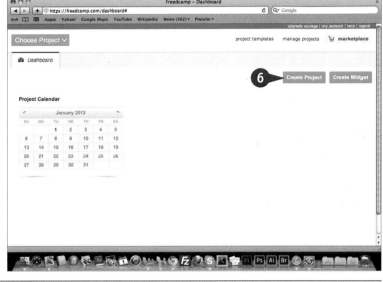

The Add Project dialog box appears.

7 Type the project name.

8 Click the **Project Group** pop-up menu and select the type of project.

9 Type a description of the project.

10 Click **Next.**

TIP

What is the different between online and desktop project management tools?
Online tools are project management applications that team members can access online without needing to install them on their desktop computers. This can enable members to manage a project from different places and devices. With the online tools, you do not have to buy a license for your team; instead you can use the free versions of project management tools or purchase monthly subscriptions. Alternatively, the desktop tools are more complex and hard to use with remote teams where members work from various places. Desktop applications that provide free project management include Gantt Project (www.ganttproject.biz). and 2-plan (http://2-plan.com).

continued ▶

Freed Camp projects give you the option to install modules known as *applications*. These applications are tools such as the To-dos list that allows you to create tasks and assign these tasks to experts on your team. The Discussions module enables you to discuss the project with the team and archive these discussions; and you use Milestones to schedule important dates in the delivery timeline for the project. You can also upload files up to 20MB and share them, and you can upgrade your account to get more storage space.

Create a Freedcamp Project (continued)

The Applications dialog box appears.

11 Click **Install** next to the application you want in the project.

12 Click **Next.**

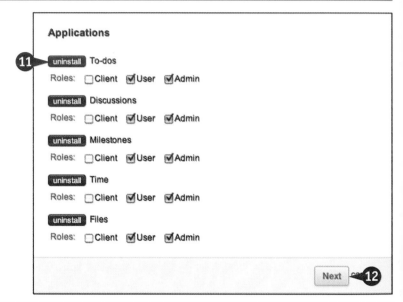

The Invitations for SEO Process dialog box appears.

13 Type the team member's e-mail address that you would like to invite to the project.

14 Click **Next.**

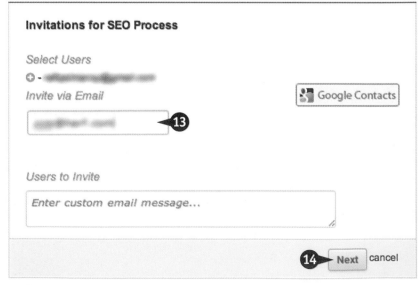

The Project Created dialog box appears.

⑮ Click **Close.**

Project Created!

Well that was easy. If you want more applications, the marketplace is filled with free and paid ones.

Freedcamp offers state of the art Bug Tracking and Invoicing! This and much more awaits you at our marketplace.

Visit the Freedcamp Marketplace

 close

⑯ Click **Choose Project.**

⑰ Click the project you created.

The project dashboard appears to let you manage it.

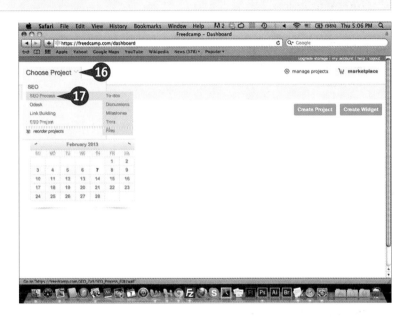

TIPS

What is the project group?

The *project group* allows you to view multiple projects under one group. When you view the projects in the Choose Project drop-down list, you will find similar projects grouped together. You can use the groups feature to arrange different SEO projects; for example, if you are running the same SEO campaign on different projects, you can group them by SEO campaign.

What are the Freedcamp widgets?

In addition to the applications that you can install for each project, you can create widgets that appear on your personal dashboard. For example, you can create a widget that displays a calendar for a specific project or all your projects. You can also create widgets such as To-dos, Activity, Bug Tracker, and Milestones.

Index

Symbols and Numerics

Index